At Issue

The Local Food Movement

Other Books in the At Issue Series:

AIDS in Developing Countries
Age of Consent
Are Athletes Good Role Models?
Are Natural Disasters Increasing?
Biodiversity
Does Outsourcing Harm America?
Does the U.S. Two-Party System Still Work?
The Energy Crisis
The Federal Budget Deficit
How Does Religion Influence Politics?
Is Iran a Threat to Global Security?
Is There a New Cold War?
Nuclear and Toxic Waste
Piracy on the High Seas
The Right to Die
Should the Federal Government Bail Out Private Industry?
Should the Internet Be Free?
Should the U.S. Close Its Borders?
Should Vaccinations Be Mandatory?
Voter Fraud

At Issue

The Local Food Movement

Amy Francis, Book Editor

GREENHAVEN PRESS
A part of Gale, Cengage Learning

Detroit • New York • San Francisco • New Haven, Conn • Waterville, Maine • London

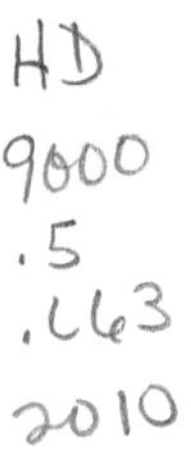

Christine Nasso, *Publisher*
Elizabeth Des Chenes, *Managing Editor*

For more information, contact:
Greenhaven Press
27500 Drake Rd.
Farmington Hills, MI 48331-3535
Or you can visit our Internet site at gale.cengage.com

Articles in Greenhaven Press anthologies are often edited for length to meet page requirements. In addition, original titles of these works are changed to clearly present the main thesis and to explicitly indicate the author's opinion. Every effort is made to ensure that Greenhaven Press accurately reflects the original intent of the authors. Every effort has been made to trace the owners of copyrighted material.

LIBRARY OF CONGRESS CATALOGING-IN-PUBLICATION DATA

The local food movement / Amy Francis, book editor.
p. cm. -- (At issue)
Includes bibliographical references and index.
ISBN 978-0-7377-4888-8 (hardcover) -- ISBN 978-0-7377-4889-5 (pbk.)
1. Farm produce--Marketing--Juvenile literature. 2. Family farms--Juvenile literature. 3. Farmers' markets--Juvenile literature. 4. Organic farming--Juvenile literature. I. Francis, Amy.
HD9000.5.L63 2010
338.1--dc22
2010000265

Printed in the United States of America
1 2 3 4 5 6 7 14 13 12 11 10

Contents

Introduction

Although it receives little media or public attention when it is reviewed in Congress about every five years, the farm bill has an enormous impact on the daily lives of Americans and the lives of those around the globe. It influences which foods are available to people in supermarkets and school cafeterias, the survival or failure of small farms, the preservation of U.S. forests, the sustainability of U.S. farmland, and even impacts the price of grain and the success of farmers in countries who import crops.

Frequently thought of as the first farm bill, the Agricultural Adjustment Act of 1933 was created with the goal of aiding farmers hurt by the Great Depression. The legislation provided farmers with incentives not to farm a portion of their land in an effort to reduce the supply of some commodity crops in order to raise their value on the market. This legislation eventually had the desired effect of helping small farms to succeed without turning to large commodity crops and enabled better environmental practices by essentially paying farmers for what they did not grow.

The farm bill however has changed dramatically through its years of revision in Congress, and eventually the U.S. government began paying farmers instead for what they did grow. In fact, by 2002, the farm bill no longer supported small farms growing produce; instead, it used subsidies to encourage the overproduction of only five commodities, including corn (frequently used as a sweetener) and soy. Although some point out the benefits of this policy, including allowing large farms to operate more efficiently and providing surplus food in the form of aid to other countries, critics have argued that this policy is flawed.

Michael Pollan pointed out in a 2007 *New York Times Magazine* article, written while the farm bill was before Congress, that the least expensive foods, calorie for calorie, tend to be processed foods. He explains, "The reason the least healthful calories in the supermarket are the cheapest is that those are the ones the farm bill encourages farmers to grow." This not only means that low-income people have fewer healthy options in the grocery store, but it also affects what is served by organizations such as public school cafeterias, which operate under tight budgets.

In a 2007 article for the *Boston Globe*, Hugh Joseph also pointed out the problems with the existing farm bill, writing, "While 39 percent of all U.S. farmers and ranchers received crop subsidies in 2005, very few were fruit and vegetable farmers. . . . Between 1985 and 2000 the real price of fruits and vegetables increased by 40 percent while the price of soft drinks and other sugary and high-fat foods declined by as much as 20 percent, thanks to massive federal subsidies for corn and soybean producers."

However, with the latest version of the farm bill, known as the Food, Conservation, and Energy Act of 2008, these critics may have reason to be encouraged. The rise of the local food movement, the organic food industry, and environmental concerns did not escape those working on this latest revision. The new farm bill reflects a change, however small, toward a food policy that supports small farms, more sustainable food production, nutrition programs, and environmental conservation.

Although commodity crops remained well funded, their funding was reduced, and funding for nutrition programs, including expanding the Fresh Fruit and Vegetable Program, which helps put fresh food in school cafeterias, was increased. In fact, nutrition programs now make up more than 67 percent of total farm bill spending. New funding was also marked to help those farmers who wish to transition to organic methods, and funding was added to support the growth of farm markets.

While some are hopeful these changes mark a turn in the government's food policy, many others feel the latest farm bill did not go far enough and point to the still large amount of funding for commodity crops. The *Anniston Star*, a daily newspaper in Alabama, published an opinion on June 11, 2008, shortly after the bill was passed, stating, "This farm bill is a hodgepodge of good and bad. It is a crying shame that the United States continues to subsidize agribusiness when most elements in it are making money hand over fist while the small farmer, the family farmer, is struggling with high fuel and production costs."

Oxfam America, an international relief and development organization, also reacted to the new farm bill in a press release dated May 9, 2008, pointing out, "While accomplishing little reform, the final bill does make incremental improvements by increasing nutrition and conservation funding and providing a host of critical provisions beneficial to socially disadvantaged producers here at home."

In the end, the farm bill will continue to be revisited every five years, next in 2012, and public demand for fresh and local foods, the economic sustainability of farms both large and small, the environmental impact of farming, and the global food market are all likely to be debated once again. These and other issues are explored by the authors in *At Issue: The Local Food Movement.*

1

Local Eating Is Growing in Popularity

Carol Smith

Carol Smith has a degree in journalism and has held various communications posts, including coordinating the editorial team at the Commission for Environmental Cooperation in her hometown of Montreal. She currently resides in Tokyo where she works to promote sustainable living with the United Nations University Media Studio.

As people give more thought to what they consume, many are taking the desire to live more simply to the market. This is evidenced in the growing popularity of farm markets as well as in urban, backyard, and community gardening endeavors, and even in the practice of foraging for wild food in local forested lands. These trends can be seen across the globe. Although growing a large sustainable garden is not feasible for everyone, there are still many choices individuals can make that are both healthy for their bodies and better for the environment. Simply learning about the food we eat is the first step.

Quite an old concept, and one ascribed to by such notable persons as Mahatma Gandhi and naturalist Henry David Thoreau, "voluntary simplicity" is making a comeback in the global North.

With climate change and oil depletion issues looming large and recession hitting hard, more people are realizing that our way of life is unnecessarily resource-intensive.

Rethinking Food Sources

Of particular concern to such "slow livers" or "downshifters" in rich industrialised countries is their reliance on a food system that is dependent on massive fossil fuel inputs. (Not to mention the health impacts of a diet based on chemical-drenched produce, processed foods and hormone-filled animal products).

Truly tackling the problem would, according to the Post Carbon Institute, require a "systematic reinvention of the food production and delivery system" at a broad level, and perhaps the hot new [2009] documentary *Food, Inc.*, will have viewers agreeing.

Meanwhile, individuals are showing a growing personal interest in the origin and impact of their own food. Thanks to this new breed of "locavores", the North American local food movement has become surprisingly vibrant and farmers' markets are enjoying newfound popularity. The trend has also hit Japan (though this is partly due to food safety concerns after several labelling and tainted food scandals) where it is not uncommon to see a farmer's photo on the label of fresh supermarket vegetables.

Low-Impact Food

While communal and home gardens still make up only a fraction of the developed world's food supply, their popularity is also expanding, as witnessed by the astounding number of bloggers chronicling their backyard efforts towards edibles independence.

Examples of low-impact food trends include everything from balcony gardening, the Obamas-inspired rebirth of "victory gardens", to homesteading [a "back to the land" movement], guerilla gardening [gardening on land you don't own] and freeganism [which involves salvaging food that would otherwise be discarded and living an anti-consumerist lifestyle]. Here is an introduction to some interesting movements and inspiring people.

Urban Agriculture

In developing and emerging market countries, urban gardens are more an issue of food security and food justice rather than carbon footprints. However, since cities cover only 2% of the earth's surface while consuming 75% of its resources, in the global drive to lower emissions, the spread of urban agriculture to the industrialised world is essential.

These days, garden plots are hot. In Berlin, there are 80,000 urban farmers and in the UK [United Kingdom] there are wait lists for space in allotments. In the struggling ex-automotive centre of the US [United States], a "Grown in Detroit" cooperative of urban farmers are not only feeding themselves, but selling surplus produce as well.

"This need not be a marginal activity in a place like Detroit," said Michael Hamm, professor of sustainable agriculture at Michigan State University. "The possibilities for economic development become real."

In the global drive to lower emissions, the spread of urban agriculture to the industrialised world is essential.

A recent study by one of his students found that the city has enough suitable vacant land to grow 76% of the vegetables and 42% of the fruits Detroiters need for a healthy diet.

Community Gardens

City dwellers find that communal gardens not only supplement their diet but create social ties with neighbours too. As one resident told a Madrid newspaper: "Now we have something to talk about in the elevator."

Amber Westfall agrees there are added benefits. An office manager at a holistic health care clinic and budding yoga instructor, she took the plunge into growing food in the spring and now spends about six–ten hours a week at a municipal allotment in Ottawa, Canada.

"I think of the plot as my backyard," she told us in an e-mail interview last week [July 2009]. "I don't go there just to garden. I like hanging out there, reading, doing yoga, inviting friends for picnics."

The 33-year-old lives in an apartment that is a 15-minute cycle away from her 93-square-meter plot at what she describes as "an incredibly diverse place, very multicultural. Lots of new Canadians, a wide range of young and old—the Hope Garden."

Living Simply and Food Traditions

Amber has been chronicling her gardening learning curve, as well as her weekly harvests, on her blog Unstuffed, which is an interesting look at efforts to live ever more simply and resiliently. Her interest in low-impact food began when she embarked on a "Buy Nothing New" year in 2008, during which she reduced her consumption as much as possible.

"Since food was one of the few things I obviously continued to buy new, I thought about food a lot," she said. "I thought about the origin of food, how it is grown, what's in it, who or what grows it, in what conditions, how it is shipped."

She turned to food issues authors like Michael Pollan, Vandana Shiva and Wendell Berry and the Web (e.g., The Ethicurean [blog]) to educate herself. Some of whom wrote "so eloquently about the joys of eating locally and seasonally, and growing and preserving their own food" that they invoked nostalgia, and Amber found herself turning to her grandmother.

"Memories came back from when I was young, of my grandmother's lush gardens, the jams and pickles she made, the cool stone crocks of things fermenting in the basement," she explained. "I had long conversations with her about how she did all those things, rediscovered a bit of my heritage, and picked up some sage wisdom about the way things were done back in the day."

Foraging for Food

The historical record has only a handful of examples of long-term sustainable societies, all of which were based on agriculture and hunting and gathering. And since there is not yet proof of a sustainable industrial society, it is safe to assume that some knowledge of old-fashioned ways may be important. For example, skills in the gathering category come in handy when you are hungry, broke or want to lighten your foodprint even further.

Amber, for one, developed an appetite for foraged plants at a wild edibles workshop last summer. This spring she took a six-week course that taught her to recognize and harvest wild vegetables, fruits, and teas where they grow—a practice called wildcrafting. Botanist Martha Webber took Amber and fellow students trekking through local woods and fields, collecting free food they had never before noticed.

Every year, Japan throws a staggering 19 million tons of food into the garbage—more than three times the world's total food aid.

"She taught us how to identify fiddleheads, garlic mustard, linden leaf, ramps, morels [mushrooms] and more," Amber said. "Each night we finished with a wild feast, the menu depending on what we foraged earlier."

While continuing to enjoy wildcrafted dishes like steamed nettles and dandelion fritters and studying up on "wild ethics", Amber has now branched out. She is doing a year-long herbalism apprenticeship, learning which plants have medicinal value and how to prepare them.

Food Waste

Every year, Japan throws a staggering 19 million tons of food into the garbage—more than three times the world's total food aid.

"There is a lot of waste in Japan, not just food," says artist and blogger Ojisanjake (which is Japanese for Uncle Jake), who is a freegan. "I've found that people are only too happy if you help them by taking something they would otherwise throw away."

Originally from the UK, 55-year-old Jake has been in Japan for eight years after living in several countries, including five years spent with indigenous people where he says he learned a lot. A freegan "since I was a young hippie in the sixties", Jake does not rescue food (or dumpster dive) like some freegans, but says he grows a lot of his food, gets some from neighbours and occasionally buys some from locals.

"For a living, I live!" Jake replied when asked about his day job. "I find it impossible to separate out different compartments for my life . . . everything I do includes labour, leisure, education, entertainment, spirit, art, etc. I grow food, chop firewood, renovate my home, make masks, paint, write, sell a little local products, do a little tour guiding, teach a little English."

Becoming informed is the first step in comprehending the problems with industrial food production.

"I think freegan is just a new word for how we humans have lived for most of our history, i.e., cash poor," he said.

Becoming informed is the first step in comprehending the problems with industrial food production. Author Michael

Pollan's book *In Defense of Food: An Eater's Manifesto* reveals just how programmed we are in industrialised society when it comes to food.

"That anyone should need to write a book advising people to eat food could be taken as a measure of our alienation and confusion," he writes. The book examines how—instead of eating just the whole foods that our bodies need—our diet has been co-opted by science and corporations that are unnecessarily processing our food, creating myriad health issues and wasting energy.

However, knowledge is one thing and hands-on action is something else. One can start easily by cutting down on food mileage (counters are available online), finding local organic producers or farmers' markets, and by foregoing meat a few days a week (or at least learning to eat it ethically).

On the growing front, while anyone can stick a pot or two of herbs on a windowsill, city folk with no gardening experience might find anything more is too intimidating. But it doesn't have to be. . . .

It seems many agree with one blogger who said that "it is time for the consumer to step up and be responsible for what is put in their mouth."

Don't you?

2

The Local Food Movement Benefits Farms, Food Production, Environment

Pallavi Gogoi

Pallavi Gogoi is a writer for BusinessWeek Online. *She frequently writes on retailing.*

Just as small family-run, sustainable farms were losing their ability to compete in the food marketplace, the local food movement stepped in with a growing consumer demand for locally grown, organic, fresh produce. In addition to supermarket giants following the trend toward locally grown food and devoting shelf space to such items, local foods are also finding their way into schools, office cafeterias, and even prisons. Although the trend toward organic foods has not waned, consumers are increasingly aware of the environmental impact caused when organic foods must travel to find their way to the local grocery store shelf. For this and other reasons, consumers are opting instead for locally grown counterparts, choosing to eat what is available in each season in their areas rather than purchasing food that must be shipped from other regions.

Drive through the rolling foothills of the Appalachian range in southwestern Virginia and you'll come across Abingdon, one of the oldest towns west of the Blue Ridge Mountains. If it happens to be a Saturday morning, you might think there's a party going on—every week between 7 a.m.

Pallavi Gogoi, "The Rise of the 'Locavore': How the Strengthening Local Food Movement in Towns Across the U.S. Is Reshaping Farms and Food Retailing," *Business Week Online*, May 21, 2008.

and noon, more than 1,000 people gather in the parking lot on Main Street, next to the police station. This is Abingdon's farmers' market. "For folks here, this is part of the Saturday morning ritual," says Anthony Flaccavento, a farmer who is also executive director of Appalachian Sustainable Development, a nonprofit organization working in the Appalachian region of Virginia and Tennessee.

It's a relatively recent ritual. Five years ago, the farmers' market wasn't as vibrant and it attracted just nine local farmers who sold a few different kinds of veggies. Today, there's a fourfold jump, with 36 farmers who regularly show up with a dizzying array of eggplants, blueberries, pecans, home-churned butter, and meat from animals raised on the farms encircling the town. It's a sign of the times: Hundreds of farmers' markets are springing up all around the country. The U.S. Agriculture Department says the number of such markets reached 4,692 in 2006, its most recent year of data, up 50% from five years earlier. Sales from those markets reached $1 billion.

New Niches

The rise of farmers' markets—in city centers, college towns, and rural squares—is testament to a dramatic shift in American tastes. Consumers increasingly are seeking out the flavors of fresh, vine-ripened foods grown on local farms rather than those trucked to supermarkets from faraway lands. "This is not a fringe foodie culture," says Flaccavento. "These are ordinary, middle-income folks who have become really engaged in food and really care about where their food comes from."

It's a movement that is gradually reshaping the business of growing and supplying food to Americans. The local food movement has already accomplished something that almost no one would have thought possible a few years back: a revival of small farms. After declining for more than a century, the number of small farms has increased 20% in the past six years, to 1.2 million, according to the Agriculture Department.

Some are thriving. Michael Paine, 34, who started farming in 2005 on just one acre in Yamhill, Ore., today has six acres of land and 110 families who buy his lettuce, cabbage, peppers, and eggplants. "I like to surprise my families with odd varieties of tomato or an odd eggplant variety, and they love it," says Paine.

The local food movement has already accomplished something that almost no one would have thought possible a few years back: a revival of small farms.

Patrick Robinette saw a growing interest among Americans in specialty beef, and in 2001 started raising ten cows at Harris Acres farm in Pinetops, N.C. Soon his grass-fed beef was in high demand. He now raises 600 head of cattle and delivers beef to the North Carolina governor's mansion. He has standing orders from 37 restaurants, three specialty stores, and six cafeterias.

Large Retailers Act

The impact of "locavores" [as local-food proponents are known] even shows up in that Washington salute every five years to factory farming, the farm bill. The latest version passed both houses in Congress in early May and was sent on May 20 to President George W. Bush's desk for signing. Bush has threatened to veto the bill, but it passed with enough votes to sustain an override. Predictably, the overwhelming bulk of its $290 billion would still go to powerful agribusiness interests in the form of subsidies for growing corn, soybeans, and cotton. But $2.3 billion was set aside this year for specialty crops, such as the eggplants, strawberries, or salad greens that are grown by exactly these small, mostly organic farmers. That's a big bump-up from the $100 million that was earmarked for such things in the previous legislation.

Small farmers will be able to get up to 75% of their organic certification costs reimbursed, and some of them can obtain crop insurance. There's money for research into organic foods, and to promote farmers' markets. Senator Tom Harkin [D-Iowa] said the bill "invests in the health and nutrition of American children by expanding their access to farmers' markets and organic produce."

$2.3 billion was set aside this year for specialty crops, such as the eggplants, strawberries, or salad greens that are grown by exactly these small, mostly organic farmers.

The local food movement has not been lost on the giants of food retailing. Large supermarket chains like Wal-Mart (WMT), Kroger (KR), and even Whole Foods (WFMI) depend on their scale to compete. Their systems of buying, delivering, and stocking are not easily adapted to the challenges of providing local food, which by its nature involves many diverse groups of farmers. People have gotten used to eating tomatoes and strawberries at all times of the year, and many parts of the country are too cold to produce them in the winter. Thus, even Whole Foods, which bills itself as the world's leading retailer of natural and organic foods, has committed to buying from barely four local farmers at each of its stores.

Wal-Mart, which in the last couple of years ran a "Salute to America's Farmers" program, says that buying from local farmers not only satisfies customers' desires, but also fits the company's commitment to sustainability and cutting down on food transportation. However, the company admits that local farms can never take over the produce aisle completely. "It gets complicated since not every state grows apples and lettuce, and even when they do, it doesn't grow at all times of the year," said Bruce Peterson, formerly Wal-Mart's senior vice president of perishables, in an interview 17 months ago. He has since left the company.

Broad Agenda

Nonetheless, all the giants are devoting a small but growing share of shelf space to locally bought produce. Some are even inviting the farmers into the store to promote their goods. "Obviously supermarkets don't want to lose that business," says Michael Pollan, author of the best seller *The Omnivore's Dilemma: A Natural History of Four Meals.* Neither Wal-Mart nor Whole Foods will quantify how much business they get from locally grown food.

Many consumers believe that organic foods, though seemingly healthy, may still damage the environment.

The very definition of "local" food presents a ceiling of sorts for successful small farmers. If they start shipping more than 250 miles or so, they cease to be local and their appeal vanishes. The optimal solution is to locate near densely populated areas, but that's where acreage is scarce. "Land prices are very expensive around metro and urban areas, which is a barrier to entry," says Pollan. He thinks the solution will be for farmers to look for ways to farm more varieties of food.

The local food movement has many of the same hallmarks of the organic foods movement, which sprang up in the 1970s to place a premium on foods grown without pesticides and synthetic fertilizers. Indeed, almost all of today's small farmers use organic techniques. But many consumers believe that organic foods, though seemingly healthy, may still damage the environment. For instance, organic fruits that are grown in Chile and Argentina and then shipped halfway around the world require fossil fuels and carbon emissions to power tankers and trucks thousands of miles. Instead of just focusing on pesticides and chemicals, consumers who have been educated by movies like *An Inconvenient Truth* now pore over "food miles" and "carbon footprints." The message seems to be: If you buy organic, you care about your own body; if you buy local, you care about your body and the environment. As more and more consumers take those values to the store with them, the impact is being felt far from the predictable centers of "green" consciousness. In Bloomington, Ind., supermarket chains such as Kroger still dominate, but an upstart called Bloomingfoods Market that specializes in local fare lately has been stealing market share. Today the cooperative has 7,000 shopping members, up from 2,000 five years ago. It works with 180 farmers to offer everything from strawberries and persimmons to squash and shiitake mushrooms. "We're seeing a real renaissance," says Ellen Michel, marketing manager for Bloomingfoods.

As the local food movement grows more mainstream, it's showing up in unexpected places. Corporations such as Best Buy (BBY) in Minneapolis, DreamWorks (DWA) in Los Angeles, and Nordstrom (JWN) in Seattle are providing local options in their cafeterias. "We try to purchase as much as we can from farmers in a 150-mile radius," says Fedele Bauccio, CEO of Bon Appétit Management, which runs more than 400 cafeterias for companies like Oracle (ORCL) and Target (TGT).

As many as 1,200 school districts around the country, from Alabama to Iowa, have linked up with local farms to serve fresh vegetables and fruit to children.

Blossoming Interest

As many as 1,200 school districts around the country, from Alabama to Iowa, have linked up with local farms to serve fresh vegetables and fruit to children. Colleges such as Brown, Cornell, the University of Montana, and the University of California, Berkeley are buying from their state's own producers. Last year, Iowa's Woodbury County mandated that its food service supplier buy from local farmers for places where it serves food, such as its prison and detention center.

And in hundreds of towns, people are signing up for CSAs, or community supported agriculture organizations, where they pay a local farmer for a weekly supply of produce during the harvest season. In 2000, there were around 400 farms that had CSA programs; today there are more than 1,800 nationwide. Families typically pay a farm $150 to $650 each year in return for a weekly basket of vegetables, fruits, eggs, meat, or baked goods. In New York City, where 11,000 residents participate with 50 farms, the demand is so high that there's a wait list. And in some inner cities, like the Bronx, a borough of New York City, organizations are training community gardeners to grow vegetables like collard greens, herbs, and beets for their community, changing food habits in the process. "We are even teaching people how to prepare seasonal produce," says Jacquie Berger, executive director of Just Food, a nonprofit that helps fresh food growers sell to residents in the Bronx.

That may be less of an issue in more pastoral settings such as Abingdon. But residents of the Virginia town look forward to Saturday at the farmers' market, mingling, passing out petitions, and letting the kids snack on berries while their parents shop for the week's groceries in a fresh setting. "There's a groundswell of interest not just for vegetables and fruits, but also eggs, poultry, and meat—people want it close to home, as fresh as possible, and produced sustainably," says farmer Flaccavento.

3

Local Food Is Not Always the Best Choice

Pamela Cuthbert

Pamela Cuthbert is the editor of Slow Canada, *a quarterly journal for Slow Food Canada.*

While consumers flock to buy foods marked as "local," many do not realize that local food can have a bigger negative impact on the environment than buying imported food. Consumers need to consider farming practices along with a food's origin, because a food's carbon footprint depends more on how the food was raised or grown than how far it traveled from farm to shelf. Further, local foods are not necessarily grown with sustainable or organic farming methods, therefore consumers choosing local foods may not be getting what they think they are. Consumers need to consider all facets of food production in order to make informed decisions about what is best for their health, the environment, farmers, and food production employees.

Buying local foods has proven so trendy that the *New Oxford American Dictionary* named "locavore" the word of the year for 2007. "Localvore" is the spelling preferred by some. The discrepancy is a sign of how early in its evolution this concept is in spite of gangbuster popularity, especially among eco-foodies. But what precisely does "local" mean? The ideology is commonly equated with good: fewer food miles are spent on transport; local economies, including family-run farms, are supported; the environment comes out cleaner in the wash as do consumers' consciences. Imaginations run free and even the livestock, are said to lead idyllic lives. Naturally, the taste is superior. It's a tall order.

The Problem with Local Foods

Step into a big-box supermarket and you'll find produce, meats and other goods that fit the bill. But the fact is, the majority of "local" stems from the industrial model: foods grown with environment-destroying fertilizers and sprayed with pesticides that prove residual, farm to fork; animals raised in inhumane conditions using cheap labour for maximum profit and yield; genetically modified crops and more. Even the question of spared food miles is murky upon closer inspection: Locally grown foods can leave a large carbon footprint depending on the mode of transport and other conditions including storage systems.

"Do we understand what we're buying when we buy local?" asks Tomas L. Nimmo, organizer of the Guelph, Ont., organics food conference where this year's public forum, a gauge of the provocative topic du jour, was "Organic, Local, Fair Trade—All of the Above or None of the Above?" Nimmo is interested in seeing the local myth destroyed, but says it won't be easy. "Setting standards for identifying local products is tricky, beyond the distance travelled."

Locally grown foods can leave a large carbon footprint depending on the mode of transport and other conditions including storage systems.

Local Foods in the Grocery Store

Supermarkets are where most Canadians get their groceries, so I roamed the aisles of my local supermarket in search of local foods. It was surprisingly easy, even in mid-winter Ontario, to fill the shopping cart with goods that meet the national standard: The federal government's Canadian Food Inspection Agency regulates the use of "local" as generally meaning food that has travelled no more than 50 km [31 miles] from where it was grown or processed. After a quick survey of local goods on offer—from battery-bird eggs to my "local" bacon producer, Maple Leaf Foods, I settled on a dish of pork and apples to see exactly how the grub measured up to the ideology.

Marketing Local Foods

In Ontario, a number of new marketing organizations hopping aboard the local train—such as Homegrown Ontario, a year-old marketing campaign from the sheep, veal and pork farmers associations—apply the "local" label to province-wide goods. Keith Robbins is with Ontario Pork, the farmer-member alliance that represents roughly 3,000 pig farms in Ontario. He reports: The typical commercial pig farm in Ontario has roughly 6,000 sows each year, where each animal is fed on a ration of genetically modified soybean and corn that is enhanced with antibiotics and growth hormones, to a mature weight of about 250 lbs. in a period of six months. They are raised entirely indoors—a common practice in commercial pig farms starting in the 1950s—with an allowance in group pens of eight sq. feet per animal. Robbins says these intensive rearing methods are needed to compete in the marketplace. "Pork is the most consumed meat in the world," and being in the game means "lowering our costs to meet the food basket." Robbins says the buyers are particularly demanding: Canadians currently spend 10 per cent or less of their incomes on food, which is the lowest ratio anywhere.

Now to that source of local apples, which at this time of year are nice and crisp thanks to being stored in energy-sucking refrigeration systems. Growing apples on a commercial scale in Ontario is challenging, in part because wet conditions make the crops more vulnerable to pests, especially a persistent fungus called scab. So fungicides are needed. The U.S. consumer advocacy organization Environmental Working Group recommends buying organic apples since conventional ones tend to be contaminated with pesticide residues. Is this a case where buying organic—and imported—is better than buying local?

Multiple studies indicate that locally grown food can in fact leave a bigger carbon footprint than food imported from countries on the other side of the globe.

Organic Versus Local

Canadian Organic Growers head Laura Telford is tired of the "organic versus local" debate that has been raging lately, especially among leagues of ethical eaters, and feels it's best to buy both when possible. But of the conventional apple, she says organic wins hands down: "[The conventional one] has had at least seven chemical baths." True, organically grown apples are free of artificial toxins. On the other hand, they generally come with a high environmental cost: food miles, plus the fact they are commonly grown in dry, arid climates where the pests can't thrive, but the trade-off is that the orchards require extensive irrigation. Marc Xuereb of Region of Waterloo Public Health, a poster boy for the campaign against food miles, is questioning the current popularization of local. Xuereb's acclaimed 2005 study of food miles considered goods that could be grown in his area, but were imported at an average distance of 4,497 km. Today, he says, "If we want to blindly say 'buy local,' then we miss the point. We realize now the issues are certainly more than just about how far food travels and that's one of the restrictions of our report." Multiple studies indicate that locally grown food can in fact leave a bigger carbon footprint than food imported from countries on the other side of the globe. When researchers at Lincoln University in New Zealand investigated food miles, they concluded that dairy raised in New Zealand and shipped to Britain actually had a smaller carbon footprint than the U.K.'s [United Kingdom's] own dairy and argued against "the fallacy of using a simplistic concept like 'food miles' as a basis for restrictive trade and marketing policies." Xuereb says, "You have to be prepared to ask questions."

Finding Balance

Mark Cutrara buys local—with stipulations. The chef/owner of Cowbell Restaurant in downtown Toronto, a place known for its meaty menu, sources pasture-raised pigs, pharmaceutical-free, that grow to about 280 lbs. in 24 months on a farm near Stratford, Ont. "I'm winning on both fronts: I get meat with great flavour and it's a local product I can stand by," he says. "I know the animal was treated ethically."

Similarly, chef David Garcelon of the Fairmont Royal York Hotel in Toronto is selective about what he buys locally, and gets his apples from Warner Orchards in Niagara. "People actually comment on the apples here, which is surprising given all the food we serve." Farmer Jim Warner, a third-generation fruit grower who works about 140 acres of land using conventional methods, uses a system called IPM—integrated pest management—to reduce the amount of spray on his orchards. "My dad used to spray every ten days because that's what you did," he says. "Now we don't spray until we see a need for it."

Lori Stahlbrand, head of the organization Local Food Plus [LFP], pairs the words "local and sustainable" as essential cofactors. "We believe that local alone does not recognize issues of sustainability, animal welfare, labour practices, biodiversity and energy use. We want always to see those two words linked together: local and sustainable, like peanut butter and jam or research and development." LFP certifies local, participating farms on a strict set of guidelines. The company launched 18 months ago with 15 suppliers and today has 65, plus a long and ever-increasing queue of applicants. "There is definitely the demand and it outstrips the supply," says Stahlbrand. "This is such a hot topic and we are being approached daily from organizations from all over this province and [the rest of the country] as well."

As for supporting the holy grail of conscientious shopping—the triumvirate of fair trade, family farms and good labour practices—there are no guarantees that come with the local label.

The first supermarket to join LFP is an independent grocer in Toronto, Fiesta Farms. Butcher Patrick Vozzo carries it all: local, conventional meats as well as organic and LFP-certified. "We have to support our local economy," he says. "And people want it. They want local." Wayne Roberts of the Toronto Food Policy Council considers buying local from an entirely different perspective: He's worried about food security and building a reliable infrastructure of accessible foods. The city's food supply is about 5 per cent locally sourced, Roberts reports, and has about three days' worth of food access and stockpile in the case of a disaster. "What is really driving the issue [of buying local] is the food movement, not from a policy or emergency planning standpoint. I'm trying to work with that wave in a most opportunistic way and push forward my agenda."

Local Does Not Mean Better

As for supporting the holy grail of conscientious shopping—the triumvirate of fair trade, family farms and good labour practices—there are no guarantees that come with the local label. Fair trade, which is regulated internationally to ensure farmers are properly compensated, has yet to come to Canada, where small, family-operated farms are characterized by a below-zero net-income crisis. As for workers in the field, they have few rights. In Ontario, where nearly all migrant farm labourers come to work—16,500 of 20,000 in 2005—there are no unions or access to collective bargaining. This applies to all agricultural employees, something the United Food and Commercial Workers [International Union]—the same union that spearheaded the unionization of workers at Wal-Mart starting in Quebec—is lobbying to change.

"People just want simple answers," sympathizes Telford. "But there are no simple answers in agriculture. You have to take an informed approach to the food system." She sighs. "You don't want to get supermarket paralysis. I get it sometimes."

4

Buying Local Is Better for Both Local and Global Economies

Carlo Petrini

Carlo Petrini is the founder of the international Slow Food movement. In addition to numerous articles, he is also the author of Slow Food Revolution: A New Culture for Dining and Living *and* Slow Food: The Case for Taste.

Large-scale agriculture has worsened already difficult conditions for smaller farms all over the globe, and it's up to farmers, government, trade organizations, and consumers to create a new food system. The farmers already dedicated to sustainable farming practices are in the best place to oversee the creation of a new system, one that values fair wages and clean, quality food over inexpensive, high-profit, low-quality produce. To accomplish this, farmers need the broad support of the government and trade organizations. Further, the goal of aid organizations should be to help struggling regions develop their own local food production, thus helping these regions become self-sufficient while also supporting sustainable agriculture, protecting the environment, and building local economies. When agricultural aid in the form of cheap, low-quality food from wealthy nations is shipped to developing nations, it only serves to weaken the existing local farms. Finally, if every consumer committed to buying responsibly by considering whether a purchase was fairly produced and traded, it could have an enormous global impact.

Carlo Petrini, "Fair," *Slow Food Nation: Why Our Food Should Be Good, Clean, and Fair*, translated by Carla Furian and Jonathan Hunt from *Buono, Pulito e Giusto*, New York, NY: Rizzoli, 2007.

In food production, the word "fair" connotes social justice, respect for workers and their know-how, rurality and the country life, pay adequate to work, gratification in producing well, and the definitive revaluation of the small farmer, whose historical position in society has always been last.

Creating a Fair Food System

It is not acceptable that those who produce our food, those people (half the total world population) who work to grow crops, raise livestock, and turn nature into food, should be treated like social outcasts and struggle to make ends meet amid all kinds of difficulty. In different parts of the world, farmers are facing a vast range of problems: History has given them a different relationship with the countryside, but few farmers prosper (and of those lucky few, most are neither "clean" nor "good" and do not produce quality food). The global food system should be engaged in finding out what is fair for everybody, in accordance with the characteristics of the various geographical areas of the world, but at present it is only creating unfairness and terrible hardship.

Agribusiness has turned small farmers into factory workers, slaves, paupers with no hopes for the future.

Our definition of "fair" is closely linked with the crucial concepts of social and economic *sustainability*, the dependants of ecological sustainability, the missing elements in our descriptions of sustainability in the broadest sense of the term. The fair, socially speaking, means fairness for the people who work the soil, respect for those who still love it and treat it with respect, as a source of life. *La tera l'e' basa*, "the land is low," they say in Piedmont [a region of Italy]: The farmer's life is a hard one, and the conditions to which many of them have been reduced cry out for revenge. Agribusiness has turned small farmers into factory workers, slaves, paupers with no hopes for the future. Millions of farmers in the world do not even own the land they work.

Supporting Farmers

We must create a new system that will give these people due recognition for the vital role they play: We cannot do without the farmers, the *producing communities*. It is on this concept of "community," of destiny and belonging to the human race, that the new system must be founded. Starting from them, from these producing communities, we must build a world-wide network that is capable of opposing the dominant system. We must put man, the land, and food back in the center: A *human* food network which, in harmony with nature and respectful of all diversity, will promote quality: good, clean, and fair.

The Hardships Small Farmers Face

From a social point of view, "sustainable" means promoting quality of life through dignified jobs that guarantee sustenance and fair remuneration. It means guaranteeing equity and democracy all over the world, giving everyone the right to choose his or her future. There are still too many peasants, farm laborers, that are virtual slaves who work to produce food and cannot live above the poverty line in a world that can produce enough for everybody.

The small farmer can save the world from the abyss: Let us give him the chance to do so.

In Latin America, the big *fazendeiros* exploit the work of farm laborers, giving them no rights and paying them so little as to effectively reduce them to slavery. In Africa, farmers are dying of hunger; Indian peasants commit suicide, crushed by the competition of agribusiness. Agricultural production in many parts of the world is indistinguishable from industrial production before the advent of the trade unions. Peasants die on the job or leave the country to go to live in miserable conditions in huge cities like Mexico City, Lima, Saô Paulo, New Delhi, and Beijing. At the same time, farmers in the rich areas of the world who want to produce the "good" and the "clean" find it difficult to compete with the low prices, supported by subsidies, which agro-industry can afford. The system is perverse: It does not allow other models, but where will this all end? Who will produce our food?

The small farmer can save the world from the abyss: Let us give him the chance to do so.

Reinventing the Food System

We must create the conditions for a new, rebalanced global order based on social justice for those who work the land, for the real and potential custodians of our land. In the areas that have been conquered by agribusiness, we must give small producers back their dignity and encourage "clean" small-scale production. But in order to make this possible, those who exceed the limits will have to be penalized, and governments must support the birth—the rebirth—of a *new rurality*. By this I mean a countryside that is "clean" and attractive, and not only in the aesthetic sense of the word: A pleasant place to live where the quality of life is guaranteed. At present, wherever agribusiness triumphs, the countryside is a lifeless place, lacking in basic amenities (small businesses, meeting points, places where one can enjoy the beauties of nature), and often ugly. Its main function is that of a dormitory for city workers attracted by a nostalgia (which remains unsatisfied) for the country life and the fact that real estate prices are lower (not surprisingly, since there is no public transport, and everyone travels by car, congesting the city centers and making the air unbreathable). A new rurality in the rich areas: This is another prime objective.

The Role of International Organizations

In other parts of the world, where conditions are often extremely serious, pressure must be put, first of all, on organizations such as the World Trade Organization and the World Bank, which have not only heightened the problems of inequality with their commercial and economic regulations, but do their utmost to maintain the status quo. The situation is full of terrible inequalities, and I am certainly not the first person to have decried it. Secondly, we must ensure that governments, overburdened as they are with debts, begin to work seriously to achieve lasting development and will not be influenced by the agribusiness lobby, which is always making grand promises but is only interested in expanding its own market. We need international controls on the levels of corruption in certain governments, which exploit humanitarian aid to enrich themselves and contribute to the destruction of the weak domestic markets; the latter are weakened by the flood of free agricultural produce, and the collapse of the meager local production is the inevitable result. We should be providing incentives to this local production, in accordance with tradition, primarily in the interests of self-sufficiency, giving all peoples sovereignty over their own food supplies; people must be able to produce *their own* food by themselves.

We should be providing incentives to this local production, in accordance with tradition, primarily in the interests of self-sufficiency, giving all peoples sovereignty over their own food supplies.

Restoring the balance of a whole world is one of the hardest tasks imaginable, but the means by which a change of course can be made without renouncing the search for quality should be clear by now: small-scale production, self-sufficiency, crop diversification, the revival and use of traditional methods, full respect for a fruitful interaction with the local biodiversity, and agroecology.

Economic Considerations

In addition to the social point of view, in the context of "fairness" there is also an economic sustainability which needs to be assessed. I have already mentioned fair remuneration for farmers. It is not possible for one liter of olive oil to cost less than seven or eight dollars: If that does happen, it can only mean that the farmer is not being paid a fair amount, that production costs are higher than the final price, and that somewhere along the food production line unfairness must have occurred. It is not fair that the illegal Mexican immigrants who work in California should be paid a pittance. It is not fair that Indian peasants who find it difficult to produce their own vegetables should have to cope with unfair competition from subsidized Western products or from surpluses created by market dumping.

Fair Trade Can Help

The *fair trade* market from this point of view is doing a very good job; it has introduced a different approach to the food economy and should therefore be encouraged and respected, though in my view it ought to be combined with structural interventions in the producing communities and not just limited to the fixing of a fair price. Fair trade must never forget the other two aspects of quality: clean and good. Sometimes it does, and this is the worst advertisement it could give itself in its struggle to rectify the unfair conventions of the market.

[Money] must be made available to the young who want to go and cultivate the land, so as to stimulate the vitality of the countryside and restore the balance of wealth.

Ensuring Social Justice

But there is also another economic aspect, which brings us back to social justice. The global financial world, the battleground of multinationals and unfair trade, has made money an elusive and immaterial entity. Capital is not "patient"; people do not invest in businesses which guarantee social justice and the redemption of peasants, or which have a low environmental impact. A movement of money on the stock exchange can seal the fate of tens of thousands of small farmers at a stroke. We need a *slower*, more "patient" investment policy, which operates outside the classical framework of finance: sustainable models of investment for the agricultural communities, which give them time to grow without expecting immediate profits. Slowing down economics means bringing it down to earth, for the earth. The World Bank, the leading international financial organization, should take note of these problems and act accordingly. The imposition of a Western free-market, financial-economic model in countries that are structurally very different from ours has only served to burden them with crippling debts, squeezing them in a vice from which they cannot extricate themselves.

Money must be brought back down to earth, it must be made available to the young who want to go and cultivate the land, so as to stimulate the vitality of the countryside and restore the balance of wealth in the world, in a line that runs from the smallest farmer to the largest capital transfers.

The Difficulties of Obtaining and Owning Land

The idea of a return to the land presupposes that there is a real possibility of achieving it. In many parts of the world, farmers abandon the land and sell it off to landowners who practice extensive agriculture; those who hold out are besieged by the chemical pollution that "modern" methods pour into the environment around their small properties. In many countries, farmers are still waiting for agrarian reform which will make uncultivated lands available to them (as in Brazil, for example, where the movement of the Sem Terra, "the landless ones," has two million members) and create conditions in which they can cultivate their smallholdings without being crushed by the power of agribusiness. Even in the rich areas of the world, many people find it difficult to go back to the land: Young people cannot raise the money to buy land, and farmers often work on rented land on behalf of big companies, so they are unable to exert any long-term influence by practicing good, clean, and fair small-scale agriculture.

Those who produce food, those who feed humanity, are always at the bottom of the social scale.

The problem of land ownership is still serious around the world, and seeking out "fair" products also means rejecting those that are the result of productive systems which create this regrettable situation: For often those who cultivate the land cannot own it, and are not free to choose the kind of agriculture they favor.

Farmers Fall to the Bottom of the Social Scale

There is an Italian expression which aptly describes the condition of farmers throughout history: They always have been, and continue to be, *l'ultima ruota del carro*, "the last wheel of the cart," the lowest sector of society. They have worked either for landowners—as in the feudal system with its hierarchical scale, where the military and the clergy were at the top and the peasants who worked for the sustenance of all were at the bottom—or for political leaders. They have always worked for an elite that did not want to dirty its hands producing food. Whether or not they owned land, their condition has been one of subordination: The means of dominion have changed with the historical periods and the cultural contexts, but the rule of the last wheel of the cart has prevailed. Even today, the situation in which farmers find themselves is not very different. If we consider the world as a whole, this subordination manifests itself in different ways from one macro-area to another. Progress has changed the styles and techniques of "dominion," but those who produce food, those who feed humanity, are always at the bottom of the social scale.

We must, of course, distinguish between two large groups: the rich, schizophrenic West, and the developing countries, which are at the mercy of the momentous upheavals that we are currently experiencing.

Globalization has had the paradoxical effect of reviving interest in diversity and local productions.

Food Production in Wealthy Nations

The "schizophrenic" situation in that part of the world, which has solved its own food-supply problems, derives from a very particular dualism, now that class divisions have diminished almost to the point of disappearing. On the one hand, we have a few rich farmers, committed to the agro-industrial model of production, who produce vast quantities of mediocre food for people who are poor, or at least not rich. On the other hand, we have a few small farmers who struggle to produce high-quality goods and who find it impossible (except in the case of the most exclusive status symbols, such as certain wine productions) to live a dignified life, such is the pressure of the competition. The latter produce food for a rich elite, who can afford the fruits of their labor, which are sometimes distributed thousands of kilometers away.

As far as social justice is concerned, in the rich West the situation is complex: Is it fair to harm the interests of those farmers who have made money through massive and extensive production in favor of small farmers who produce quality food? In reality, however, this part of the world seems to be balancing out; we have already seen how every tendency always produces an opposite one and how globalization has had the paradoxical effect of reviving interest in diversity and local productions. It seems that this dualism is gradually diminishing, thus making room for choices based on merit: Our family food budget has significantly decreased, which means there is now a portion of our income left over that can be used to support quality products. The range of choice is expanding, and in this context, anyone who acquires food products, in full awareness of the three criteria for quality, is in a good position to bring about a change. Even subsidizing policies, which are the main source of survival for the agro-industrial system, are gradually beginning to turn toward quality, as is shown by the first tentative European steps toward a reform of the Common Agricultural Policy (CAP). Consumers' persistence in choosing good, clean, and fair products can have its effect, and it will be the task of the new gastronome [a connoisseur of good food and drink] to draw attention to this behavior in the act of purchasing—to foster knowledge, so that the system can recover its balance and return within its limits.

Food Production in Developing Nations

However, the Western world must take into account the rest of the planet: Above all, we should not expect to be able to dump the surplus of our model (which does not work anymore) in the so-called developing countries. This is not sustainable from any point of view. The developing countries must find their own way, by seeking a *food sovereignty* of their own. The most we can do is to help them and avoid looking at the problem from the Eurocentric standpoint of *conquistadores* who "discovered" America.

The developing countries, though united by the immense problems and injustices that affect them, show different levels of development in the agriculture of different areas. Africa first suffered the invasion of colonialism and was then almost left to itself and to its internal conflicts. African colonizers did not consider local gastronomies worthy of respect: They simply cancelled them out along with a form of farming, which though very basic, would have been perfectly capable of evolving of its own accord if it had been properly supported and not impeded. In other parts of the world, colonization from the agro-gastronomical point of view was less destructive and created syncretisms (such as Pan-American syncretism or that between America and Europe), which preserved part of the local agricultural cultures. But soon the agro-industrial model appeared and rapidly developing countries such as Brazil, India, and Mexico are paying the price in the form of stark polarization of the classes and areas of grinding poverty.

The Unique Problem of China

We find a different situation again in the Far East, especially in China. China seems to be the great threat to the Western world with its incessant economic growth, but we should consider the problem (whether real or imagined) from the point of view of social justice. In China, workers' rights are not respected. The level of pollution, along with the indiscriminate use of GMOs [genetically modified organisms] and of agricultural practices so noxious that they are banned in every other part of the world, show an aspect of Chinese development that few seem to take into consideration—the same problems that we used to have in the West, except that in China they are happening now and far more quickly. The harm that is being done in China in the name of development is incalculable, and the system, though nominally Communist, is in fact the embodiment of perfect capitalism: political homogeneity, uncontrolled exploitation of labor, and exploitation of the natural environment with no thought of the future. We need to promote a strong international reaction, not by increasing existing tariffs or imposing new ones, not by seeking complicity, but rather by rejecting such an unfair system and making the Chinese respect the environment and their workers. If we do not, the "Chinese threat" may become huge—not because it will deprive us of wealth, but because it will drive us even more quickly toward the precipice.

It is the new gastronome's task to assess the living conditions of millions of small farmers all over the world.

Social justice, linked with the good and the clean, must become the method of development, the only one possible. These three criteria of quality will combine differently in different parts of the world, but they remain the three cardinal points on which we must build, little by little, with new tools and with the *neo-gastronomic* attitude, a new model of growth on this planet.

The Responsibility to Evaluate the Fairness of Food Falls to the Consumer

The third of the three essential and interdependent prerequisites for a quality product is that it be *fair*—fair for man and for society. "Fair" is sustainable; it creates wealth and establishes a more equitable order among the peoples of the world. Justice is obtained by respecting man—the farmer, the craftsman—and his work. It is the new gastronome's task to assess the living conditions of millions of small farmers all over the world (but particularly those close to his home), to get to know those farmers, to support the production of the "clean" and "good" ones, guaranteeing them fair remuneration through "fair trade" prices in the most serious cases.

Should anyone be tempted to ignore the complexity of the world and consume their food irresponsibly and unfairly, indifferent to social justice, I say that the fair has become indispensable. The human elite must be made up of those who produce food, not by those who consume it by consuming the land.

Fair is respect for others; working to ensure that it is pursued by everyone is another part of our civilizing mission. This is the gastronome's concern, and it leads directly to the new gastronome, who enjoys, knows, and eats in the awareness that he must leave a better earth to future generations.

5

Organic Food and Farming Has Drawbacks

Steven Shapin

Steven Shapin is the Franklin L. Ford Professor of the History of Science at Harvard. He has authored several books on science and culture, including A Social History of Truth: Civility and Science in Seventeenth-Century England. *He is also a regular contributor to the* London Review of Books.

Many consumers who purchase organic produce believe they are supporting local small farms and sustainable agriculture. That is frequently not the case. Much of the organic produce on the market comes from large farms turning a huge profit from the organic label. Further, while a few organic companies have taken steps toward reducing their carbon footprint, shipping and farming methods often contribute more greenhouse gases and do more environmental damage than is saved by using organic methods. Finally, consumers need to understand that big-business agriculture and the use of pesticides, not local farms and organic farming methods, are necessary to solving the global food crisis.

The plastic package of Earthbound Farm baby arugula in Whole Foods was grown without synthetic fertilizers; no toxic pesticides or fumigants were used to control insect predators; no herbicides were applied to deal with weeds; no genes from other species were introduced into its genome to increase yield or pest resistance; no irradiation was used to extend its shelf life. It complies with the U.S. Department of

Steven Shapin "Paradise Sold: What Are You Buying When You Buy Organic?" *The New Yorker*, vol. 82, May 15, 2006.

Agriculture's National Organic Program, a set of standards that came into full effect in 2002 to regulate the commercial use of the word "organic." So what's the problem?

Organic Does Not Mean Local

It all depends on what you think you're buying when you buy organic. If the word conjures up the image of a small, family-owned, local operation, you may be disappointed. Like Whole Foods, Earthbound Farm is a very big business. Earthbound's founders, Drew and Myra Goodman, Manhattanites who went to college in the Bay Area, and then started a two-and-a-half-acre raspberry-and-baby-greens farm near Carmel [California] to produce food they "felt good about," are now the nation's largest grower of organic produce, with revenues for this year [2006] projected at more than $450 million. Their greens, including the arugula, are produced on giant farms in six different counties in California, two in Arizona, one in Colorado, and in three Mexican states. Earthbound grows more than seventy per cent of all the organic lettuce sold in America; big organic retailers like Whole Foods require big organic suppliers. (Earthbound actually dropped the "organic" specification when it started its mass distribution program, in 1993—even though the stuff *was* organic—because its first client, Costco, thought it might put customers off.) By 2004, Earthbound was farming twenty-six thousand acres; its production plants in California and Arizona total four hundred thousand square feet, and its products are available in supermarkets in every state of the Union. The Cannel Valley farm stand is still there, largely for public relations purposes, and is as much an icon of California's entrepreneurial roots as the Hewlett-Packard garage in downtown Palo Alto.

Evaluating the Carbon Footprint

Success is not necessarily a sin, of course, and, for many people, buying organic is a way of being environmentally sensitive. Earthbound notes that its farming techniques annually obviate the use of more than a quarter of a million pounds of toxic chemical pesticides and almost 8.5 million pounds of synthetic fertilizers, which saves 1.4 million gallons of the petroleum needed to produce those chemicals. Their tractors even use biodiesel fuel.

Yet the net benefit of all this to the planet is hard to assess. Michael Pollan [author of *The Omnivore's Dilemma: A Natural History of Four Meals*], who thinks that we ought to take both a wider and a deeper view of the social, economic, and physical chains that deliver food to fork, cites a Cornell [University] scientist's estimate that growing, processing, and shipping one calorie's worth of arugula to the East Coast costs fifty-seven calories of fossil fuel. The growing of the arugula is indeed organic, but almost everything else is late-capitalist business as usual. Earthbound's compost is trucked in; the salad-green farms are models of West Coast monoculture, laser-leveled fields facilitating awesomely efficient mechanical harvesting; and the whole supply chain from California to Manhattan is only four per cent less gluttonous a consumer of fossil fuel than that of a conventionally grown head of iceberg lettuce—though Earthbound plants trees to offset some of its carbon footprint. "Organic," then, isn't necessarily "local," and neither "organic" nor "local" is necessarily "sustainable." . . .

The growing of the arugula is indeed organic, but almost everything else is late-capitalist business as usual.

Organic May Not Be Better

According to Samuel Fromartz, ninety per cent of "frequent" organic buyers think they're buying better "health and nutrition." They may be right. If, for any reason, you don't want the slightest pesticide residue in your salad, or you want to ensure that there are no traces of recombinant bovine somatotropin hormone (rBST) in your children's milk, you're better off spending the extra money for organically produced food. But scientific evidence for the risks of such residues is iffy, as it is, too, for the benefits of the micro-nutrients that are said to be more plentiful in an organic carrot than in its conventional equivalent.

Other people are buying taste, but there's little you can say about other people's taste in carrots and not much more you can intelligibly articulate about your own. The taste of an heirloom carrot bought five years ago from the Chino family farm in Rancho Santa Fe, California, sticks indelibly in my memory, though at the time I hadn't any idea whether artificial fertilizers or pesticides had been applied to it. (I later learned that they had not.) For many fruits and vegetables, freshness, weed control, and the variety grown may be far more important to taste than whether the soil in which they were grown was dosed with ammonium nitrate. Pollan did his own taste test by shopping at Whole Foods for an all-organic meal: Everything was pretty good, except for the six-dollar bunch of organic asparagus, which had been grown in Argentina, air-freighted six thousand miles to the [United] States, and immured for a week in the distribution chain. Pollan shouldn't have been surprised that it tasted like "cardboard." . . .

Following Food from Farm to Table

The quest for the shortest possible chain between producer and consumer is the narrative dynamic of Michael Pollan's book, which is cleverly structured around four meals, each representing a different network of relations between producers, eaters, and the environment, and each an attempt at greater virtue than the last. Pollan's first meal is fast food, and he follows a burger back to vast monocultural industrial blocs of Iowan corn, planted by GPS-guided tractors and dosed with tons of synthetic fertilizer, whose massive runoff into the Mississippi River—as much as 1.5 million tons of nitrogen a year—winds up feeding algal blooms and depleting the oxygen needed by other forms of life in the Gulf of Mexico. Pollan then follows the corn to enormous feedlots in Kansas, where a heifer that he bought in South Dakota is speed-fattened—fourteen pounds of corn for each pound of edible beef—for which its naturally grass-processing rumen was not designed, requiring it to be dosed with antibiotics, which breed resistant strains of bacteria. Pollan would have liked to follow his heifer through the industrial slaughterhouse, but the giant beef-packing company was too canny to let him in, and so we are spared the stomach-churning details, which, in any case, were minutely related a few years ago in Eric Schlosser's *Fast Food Nation*. Pollan also follows the American mountains of industrial corn into factories, where the wonders of food technology transform it into the now ubiquitous high-fructose corn syrup, which sweetens the soda that, consumed in super-sized quantities across the nation, contributes to the current epidemic of type 2 diabetes. All very bad things.

The Organic Label

The second meal is the Big Organic one that he bought at his local Whole Foods store in California, featuring an "organic" chicken whose "free-range" label was authorized by USDA [U.S. Department of Agriculture] statutes, but which actually shared a shed with twenty thousand other genetically identical birds. Two small doors in the shed opened onto a patch of grass, but they remained shut until the birds were five or six weeks old, and two weeks later Pollan's "free-range" chicken was a $2.99-a-pound package in his local Whole Foods. This meal was better—the corn-and-soybean chicken feed was certified organic and didn't contain antibiotics—but still not perfect. Pollan's third meal was even more virtuous. After spending several weeks doing heavy lifting on a polycultural, sustainable smallholding in the Shenandoah Valley, Pollan cooked a meal wholly made up of ingredients that he himself had a hand in producing: eggs from (genuinely) free-range, grub-eating hens, corn grown with compost from those happy birds, and, finally, a chicken whose throat he had slit himself. Very good, indeed—and no nitrogenous runoff, and no massive military machine to protect America's supplies of Middle East oil and the natural gas needed to make the synthetic fertilizer.

A Perfect Meal

Finally, Pollan decides to eat a meal—"the perfect meal"—for which he had almost total personal responsibility: wild morels [mushrooms] foraged in the Sierra [Nevada] foothills, the braised loin and leg of a wild pig he had shot himself in Sonoma County, a chamomile tisane made from herbs picked in the Berkeley Hills, salad greens from his own garden, cherries taken by right of usufruct from a neighbor's tree, sea salt scraped from a pond at the southern end of San Francisco Bay, and—O.K., strict perfection is unobtainable—a bottle of California Petite Sirah, presumably organic. This was not a way of eating that Pollan thinks is realistic on a routine basis, but he wanted to test what it felt like to have "a meal that is eaten in full consciousness of what it took to make it." That consciousness, for Pollan, is more religious than political—every meal a sacrament. "We eat by the grace of nature, not industry, and what we're eating is never anything more or less than the body of the world," he says.

Becoming Educated About the Source of Food

Pollan winds up demanding that we know much more about what we're putting into our mouths: "What it is we're eating: Where it came from. How it found its way to our table. And what, in a true accounting, it really cost." The "naked lunch," William Burroughs wrote, is the "frozen moment when everyone sees what is on the end of every fork." Burroughs meant it metaphorically; Pollan means it literally. He wants to know his farmer's name, and to know that his hamburger was once part of the muscles of a particular cow. He wants to do his bit to save the planet. That means he wants to eat locally, within a network of familiarity. But, even so, the knowledge required is potentially infinite. What particular bacteria, fungi, and trace elements lurk in the soil of your sustainable community farm? Does your friendly local farmer use a tractor or a horse? If a tractor, does it use fuel made from biomass? If a horse, are the oats it eats organic? If the oats are organic, does the manure with which they were grown come from organically fed animals? How much of this sort of knowledge can you digest?

Genetically modified, industrially produced monocultural corn is what feeds victims of an African famine, not the gorgeous organic Technicolor Swiss chard from your local farmers' market.

The Global Hunger Crisis

Pollan seems aware of the contradictions entailed in trying to eat in this rigorously ethical sprat, but he doesn't give much space to the most urgent moral problem with the organic ideal: how to feed the world's population. At the beginning of the twentieth century, there was a serious scare about an imminent Malthusian[1] crisis: The world's rapidly expanding population was coming up against the limits of agricultural productivity. The Haber-Bosch process[2] averted disaster, and was largely responsible for a fourfold increase in the world's food supply during the twentieth century. Earl Butz, [President Richard] Nixon's secretary of agriculture, was despised by organic farmers, but he might not have been wrong when he

1. After the theories of Thomas R. Malthus, who believed that unchecked, population increases at a faster rate than its means of subsistence.
2. The process by which ammonia is produced; fertilizer is generated from ammonia.

said, in 1971, that if America returned to organic methods "someone must decide which fifty million of our people will starve!" According to a more recent estimate, if synthetic fertilizers suddenly disappeared from the face of the earth, about two billion people would perish.

Supporters of organic methods maintain that total food-energy productivity per acre can be just as high as with conventional agriculture, and that dousings of N-P-K [nitrogen, phosphorous, and potassium fertilizers] are made necessary only by the industrial scale of modern agriculture and its long-chain systems of distribution. Yet the fact remains that, to unwind conventional agriculture, you would have to unwind some highly valued features of the modern world order. Given the way the world now is, sustainably grown and locally produced organic food is expensive. Genetically modified, industrially produced monocultural corn is what feeds the victims of an African famine, not the gorgeous organic Technicolor Swiss chard from your local farmers' market. Food for a "small planet" will, for the foreseeable future, require a much smaller human population on the planet.

Finding Food Perspective

Besides, for most consumers that Earthbound Farm organic baby arugula from Whole Foods isn't an opportunity to dismantle the infrastructures of the modern world; it's simply salad. Dressed with a little Tuscan extra-virgin olive oil, a splash of sherry vinegar, some shavings of Parmigiano-Reggiano [cheese], and fleur de sel [sea salt] from the Camargue [western Europe's largest river delta], it makes a very nice appetizer. To insist that we are consuming not just salad but a vision of society isn't wrong, but it's biting off more than most people are able and willing to chew. Cascadian Farm's Gene Kahn, countering the criticism that by growing big he had sold out, volunteered his opinion on the place that food has in the average person's life: "This is just lunch for most people. *Just lunch*. We can call it sacred, we can talk about Communion, but it's just lunch."

6

Buying Local Food Protects Regional Flavors and Traditions

Gary Paul Nabhan

Gary Paul Nabhan is cofounder of Renewing America's Food Traditions, an alliance that works to promote and ensure America's food traditions. He is also the author of two books: Coming Home to Eat: The Pleasures and Politics of Local Food *and* Why Some Like It Hot: Food, Genes, and Cultural Diversity.

Before the emergence of the local food movement, the heritage plants that produce unique varieties of many familiar fruits and vegetables were quickly disappearing from the planet. Along with these plants, the flavors unique to each region of the United States were being lost to large industrial farms that tend to rely on single varieties to turn a larger profit. A renewed interest in persevering local flavors as well as supporting small farms and reducing the carbon footprint left by increasing food miles are helping to save these unique heritage foods and regional flavors. As the global market affects food production and sales, preserving local foods is no easy task, but it is possible. The future of local food is strong as consumers realize their options and the importance of eating local.

One recent Sunday, I ate dinner at a community center on a Navajo reservation in Leupp, Arizona, not far from the Grand Falls of the Little Colorado River. A heavy fog had

Gary Paul Nabhan, "How Green Is Our Valley; Networks of Local Food Growers, Restaurants, and Farmers' Markets Promote the Joys of Regional Cuisine: Flavor, Prosperity, and the Family Farm," *On Earth*, vol. 71, March 22, 2005, pp. 12–13.

settled over the Painted Desert, but as we sat down to our meal, the fog lifted, revealing the dusty soil from which the foods we were about to eat had been grown and harvested. We relished a savory posole stew of hominy mixed with Navajo-Churro lamb that had grazed on native herbs and was imbued with the distinctive taste of wild sage. The stew was served with moist, flavorful blue corn bread and a delectable baked Blue Hubbard squash, a local heirloom pumpkin.

Bringing Heirloom Foods Back to the Table

The makings of our feast included some of the 700 "heritage foods" traditionally cultivated across the North American continent: foods that, until recently, had nearly vanished. Now many are being put back on the tables of restaurants and banquet halls near where they are grown and are being used to create distinctive regional cuisines. Our Navajo meal was not an isolated event or some exotic, faddish happening. It was part of a concerted effort to conserve regionally adapted seeds and animal breeds and to renew native and immigrant food traditions here and around the country, from the waters of the Louisiana bayous to the maple forests of Vermont's Green Mountains.

In 2002, for the first time in history, the United States—long considered the breadbasket to the world—imported more food than it exported.

The Growing Popularity of Local Foods

In northern Arizona, where I live, a coalition of conservation and agriculture groups called Renewing America's Food Traditions has been funding events like the Navajo banquet for the past two years. Promoting foods that reflect the region's history and environment is part of a larger goal of encouraging sustainable farming, fostering land preservation, and boosting economic vitality.

Regional culinary treasures—sometimes called place-based foods—have found their way into high-end restaurants in Santa Fe, Los Angeles, New York, and other cosmopolitan centers. But on that foggy Sunday night at the Navajo reservation, in an area where poverty rates are more than twice the national average (due in part to a crippling seven-year drought), we sat on folding chairs and ate off card tables in a wind-battered community center. If locally grown foods can bring environmental and economic benefits to this struggling region—and that is happening—they can do the same for the rest of the country.

Finding Local Foods in a Global Market

In theory, purchasing food from local producers should be simple. It once was. But today's factory farms funnel their products into a global transportation network that carries the food we eat an average distance of 1,200 miles from the field to the supermarket shelf. These days, we're shipping and flying more and more of our food from overseas. In 2002, for the first time in history, the United States—long considered the breadbasket to the world—imported more food than it exported. Despite this troubling trend, it is not easy to persuade grocery store managers and restaurant chefs to change their ingrained buying habits.

Canyon Country Fresh, a campaign that I helped launch as director of the Center for Sustainable Environments at Northern Arizona University, was designed to help overcome this resistance. Our staff seeks out ranchers willing to direct-market their meat and connects them with small-scale slaughterhouses, butcher shops, market managers, caterers, and restaurant chefs. We give restaurants incentives to serve local foods by helping them figure out how to get goods delivered from the farm to their door, by educating their customers about the added value of these foods, and by publicizing their efforts (for free) in regional food directories. In Arizona, John

Sharpe of the Turquoise Room in Winslow, and Richard Fernandez of Pesto Brothers Piazza in Flagstaff, are among more than a dozen restaurant owners and chefs who have created menus using meats and produce from farms located within a few hundred miles of their establishments. Canyon Country Fresh also organizes community gatherings where chefs speak with farmers about freshness and quality assurance—the things that keep their restaurant patrons coming back for more.

Local food networks yield numerous environmental benefits. Limiting the distance food travels from producer to consumer significantly reduces transportation costs, fossil fuel consumption, and carbon emissions. Smaller, family-run farms tend to adopt sustainable farming practices more readily than do large operations. I raise Navajo-Churro sheep near Winona, Arizona, where most ranchers graze their animals in summer pastures and feed them supplemental hay in the winter, avoiding the nitrate pollution and antibiotic use associated with feedlots. Much of the grass-fed meat raised in our area is not officially certified as organic under the United States Department of Agriculture's new standards, but producers tell me that their animals are raised without any genetically engineered grains in their feed and without growth hormones. My Navajo neighbors know the history of the Churro breed and its importance to their culture. They know each and every one of their sheep by name.

Limiting the distance food travels from producer to consumer significantly reduces transportation costs, fossil fuel consumption, and carbon emissions.

Marketing Local Foods

Is there a real market for place-based foods, one that would make this model economically viable? Absolutely. It's already taking shape. Four years ago, the amount of food grown in northern Arizona and marketed in the Flagstaff area generated less than $20,000 in retail sales annually. In 2004, farmers and ranchers living within 150 miles of the city sold nearly $500,000 worth of food to our community. Since 1994, the number of farmers' markets in the United States has doubled, to more than 3,700. The natural foods industry—a vague term that includes local and organic products—is growing at a healthy rate of about 24 percent a year. Although the "buy local" movement is not ready to eclipse Wal-Mart—the world's largest food retailer raked in about $66 billion in food sales in 2004—its growth is nonetheless significant.

In northern Arizona, the economic benefits of these initiatives ripple through the community, generating more local wealth (the opposite of the Wal-Mart effect). Several years ago, I invited Francisco Perez, a renowned Spanish chef who had "retired" to the area, to lead a cooking demonstration at the Flagstaff Community Farmers' Market. Consumers raved about his pestos made from wild, locally cultivated heirloom greens and asked him to offer them at the market regularly. He now sells his pestos and sauces in area stores as well. Perez often caters "wild foods" dinners with as many as 200 attendees, exposing the uninitiated to a variety of greens, berries, and grains harvested within a 50-mile range. Perez can't do this alone: He hires at least a dozen local residents to collect his wild-food ingredients.

The Unique Needs of Each Region

Not everyone can achieve Perez's success; there is no standard recipe that's guaranteed to work. Ranchers in the Southwest, lobstermen in Maine, and growers of Cracker cattle (a relative of the Texas longhorn) in the Florida swamplands all face different challenges. Gilfeather turnip farmers in Vermont face climatic constraints unlike those that affect producers of pasture-raised heritage turkeys in New Mexico. Each region has to develop a strategy suited to its geography and culinary traditions. The Vermont Fresh Network, for instance, helps restaurants create seasonal menus that feature more root crops and aged cheeses in the winter, and more fresh greens and fruits in the summer. And the Pacific Northwest's Salmon-Safe organization works to connect grocery store managers with salmon suppliers who harvest their fish in ways that reduce stream pollution and foster the resurgence of wild salmon in the Columbia River watershed.

The Future of Local Foods

What might this forward-looking food network look like in ten years? First, many more local foods will be grown, sold, and eaten. Markets in each part of the country will be stocked with cheeses, wines, fruits, and vegetables naturally infused with distinctive flavors unique to that place. Each local food network will celebrate its own version of what the French call terroir: the special geographic, geological, climatic, and environmental attributes that affect the very growth, flavor, and fragrance of heritage products. And stronger, more prosperous regional food cooperatives across the United States will trade with one another for those specialty items—maple syrup, mesquite flour, smoked salmon, or spices, for example—that simply can't be produced in other climates.

Americans can once again take control of their food future, rather than remain victims of a globalized food system that offers fewer choices and imposes a costly environmental and social burden.

Most important, we will see a larger portion of every consumer dollar returning to farmers or ranchers rather than to middlemen, allowing producers to reinvest in rural land conservation and restoration. The mayor of Burlington, Vermont, has pledged that 10 percent of city food purchases will come from local sources within the next five years.

Of course, the very best part of such a green future is that it will taste much better and be far more memorable than one in which every meal—from New York to Los Angeles—tastes like every other meal. It is unfortunate that it has taken us so long to realize that truly pleasurable eating is so intimately linked with a stronger sense of food democracy. Americans can once again take control of their food future, rather than remain victims of a globalized food system that offers fewer choices and imposes a costly environmental and social burden.

How to Buy Local

Find out where to buy local, sustainably grown foods through Local Harvest, a nonprofit online resource that connects consumers with more than 7,000 retailers. Search for farmers' markets, grocery stores, food co-ops, restaurants, and farms offering food "subscriptions" (remember the milkman?) in your hometown: www.localharvest.org.

Help revive seeds, breeds, and heritage foods in your own community by connecting with Renewing America's Food Traditions. The organization invites everyone to nominate culturally significant foods from their area—from apples to shellfish—for the "Ark of Taste" list of endangered gastronomic treasures.

7

Local Food Is Not Necessarily Better for the Environment

Sarah DeWeerdt

Sarah DeWeerdt is a writer based in Seattle, Washington. She specializes in biology and environmental topics.

Many consumers are opting to buy local food to reduce environmental damage caused by food miles—the distance food travels from farm to consumer. However, food miles make up only a small percentage of the total greenhouse gas emissions created by farming. Farming practices, such as pesticide use and the type of food produced, have a greater impact on the environment than food miles alone. For example, animals naturally produce large amounts of methane, contributing more greenhouse gases to the atmosphere than transportation creates; therefore, consuming fewer animal products can have a larger positive impact on the environment than buying local. Food miles are just one of many factors consumers should consider when trying to make ethical food purchases.

In 1993, a Swedish researcher calculated that the ingredients of a typical Swedish breakfast—apple, bread, butter, cheese, coffee, cream, orange juice, sugar—traveled a distance equal to the circumference of the earth before reaching the Scandinavian table. In 2005, a researcher in Iowa found that the milk, sugar, and strawberries that go into a carton of strawberry yogurt collectively journeyed 2,211 miles (3,558 kilometers) just

Sarah DeWeerdt, "Is Local Food Better? Yes, Probably—But Not in the Way Many People Think," *World Watch Magazine*, vol. 22, no. 3, May–June 2009, pp. 6–10.

to get to the processing plant. As the local food movement has come of age, this concept of "food miles" (or "kilometers")—roughly, the distance food travels from farm to plate—has come to dominate the discussion, particularly in the United States, the United Kingdom, and parts of Western Europe.

The concept offers a kind of convenient shorthand for describing a food system that's centralized, industrialized, and complex almost to the point of absurdity. And, since our food is transported all those miles in ships, trains, trucks, and planes, attention to food miles also links up with broader concerns about the emissions of carbon dioxide [CO_2] and other greenhouse gases from fossil fuel-based transport.

Transporting Our Food

In the United States, the most frequently cited statistic is that food travels 1,500 miles on average from farm to consumer. That figure comes from work led by Rich Pirog, the associate director of the Leopold Center for Sustainable Agriculture at Iowa State University. (He is also behind the strawberry yogurt calculations referenced above). In 2001, in some of the country's first food miles research, Pirog and a group of researchers analyzed the transport of 28 fruits and vegetables to Iowa markets via local, regional, and conventional food distribution systems. The team calculated that produce in the conventional system—a national network using semitrailer trucks to haul food to large grocery stores—traveled an average of 1,518 miles (about 2,400 kilometers). By contrast, locally sourced food traveled an average of just 44.6 miles (72 kilometers) to Iowa markets.

In light of such contrasts, the admonition to "eat local" just seems like common sense. And indeed, at the most basic level, fewer transport miles do mean fewer emissions. Pirog's team found that the conventional food distribution system used four to 17 times more fuel and emitted five to 17 times more CO_2 than the local and regional (the latter of which roughly meant Iowa-wide) systems. Similarly, a Canadian study estimated that replacing imported food with equivalent items locally grown in the Waterloo, Ontario, region would save transport-related emissions equivalent to nearly 50,000 metric tons of [CO_2] or the equivalent of taking 16,191 cars off the road.

One problem with trying to determine whether local food is greener is that there's no universally accepted definition of local food.

Defining Local

But what exactly is "local food" in the first place? How local is local?

One problem with trying to determine whether local food is greener is that there's no universally accepted definition of local food. Alisa Smith and J.B. MacKinnon, authors of *The 100-Mile Diet: A Year of Local Eating*, write that they chose this boundary for their experiment in eating locally because "a 100-mile radius is large enough to reach beyond a big city and small enough to feel truly local. And it rolls off the tongue more easily than the '160-kilometer diet.'" Sage Van Wing, who coined the term "locavore" with a friend when she was living in Marin County, California, was inspired to eat local after reading *Coming Home to Eat: The Pleasures and Politics of Local Foods*, a chronicle of author Gary Paul Nabhan's own year-long effort to eat only foods grown within 250 miles of his northern Arizona home. She figured that if Nabhan could accomplish that in the desert, she could do even better in the year-round agricultural cornucopia that is northern California, so she decided to limit herself to food from within 100 miles.

There's some evidence that a popular understanding of local food is, at least in some places, coalescing around this 100-

mile limit. A 2008 Leopold . . . [Center for Sustainable Agriculture] survey of consumers throughout the United States found that two-thirds considered local food to mean food grown within 100 miles. Still, a variety of other definitions also persist. Sometimes local means food grown within a county, within a state or province, or even, in the case of some small European nations, within the country. In the United Kingdom, reports Tara Garnett of the Food Climate Research Network, "on the whole, organizations supporting local are now less likely to put numbers on things." Meanwhile, rural sociologist Clare Hinrichs, of Pennsylvania State University, has found that in Iowa local has shifted from signifying food grown within a county or a neighboring one to food grown anywhere in the state. For some in the agricultural community, promoting and eating "local Iowa food" is almost a kind of food patriotism, aimed at counteracting the forces of globalization that have put the state's family farmers at risk.

All of those are perfectly valid ways of thinking about local. But they don't have all that much to do with environmental costs and benefits.

Local Isn't Always Better

In any case, warns Pirog, food miles/kilometers don't tell the whole story. "Food miles are a good measure of how far food has traveled. But they're not a very good measure of the food's environmental impact."

That impact depends on how the food was transported, not just how far. For example, trains are ten times more efficient at moving freight, ton for ton, than trucks are. So you could eat potatoes trucked in from 100 miles away, or potatoes shipped by rail from 100 miles away, or potatoes shipped by rail from 1,000 miles, and the greenhouse gas emissions associated with their transport from farm to table would be roughly the same.

The environmental impact of food also depends on how it is grown. Swedish researcher Annika Carlsson-Kanyama led a study that found it was better, from a greenhouse gas perspective, for Swedes to buy Spanish tomatoes than Swedish tomatoes, because the Spanish tomatoes were grown in open fields while the local ones were grown in fossil fuel-heated greenhouses.

That seems obvious, but there are subtler issues at play as well. For example, Spain has plenty of the warmth and sunshine that tomatoes crave, but its main horticultural region is relatively arid and is likely to become more drought-prone in the future as a result of global climate change. What if water shortages require Spanish growers to install energy-intensive irrigation systems? And what if greenhouses in northern Europe were heated with renewable energy?

A broader, more comprehensive picture of all the trade-offs in the food system requires tracking greenhouse gas emissions through all phases of a food's production, transport, and consumption.

Why Consumers Focus on Food Miles

Perhaps it's inevitable that we consumers gravitate to a focus on food miles—the concept represents the last step before food arrives on our tables, the part of the agricultural supply chain that's most visible to us. And indeed, all other things being equal, it's better to purchase something grown locally than the same thing grown far away. "It is true that if you're comparing exact systems, the same food grown in the same way, then obviously, yes, the food transported less will have a smaller carbon footprint," Pirog says.

But a broader, more comprehensive picture of all the trade-offs in the food system requires tracking greenhouse gas emissions through all phases of a food's production, transport, and consumption. And life cycle analysis (LCA), a research method that provides precisely this "cradle-to-grave" perspective, reveals that food miles represent a relatively small slice of the greenhouse gas pie.

In a paper published last year, Christopher Weber and H. Scott Matthews, of Carnegie Mellon University, wove together data from a variety of U.S. government sources into a comprehensive life cycle analysis of the average American diet. According to their calculations, final delivery from producer or processor to the point of retail sale accounts for only 4 percent of the U.S. food system's greenhouse gas emissions. Final delivery accounts for only about a quarter of the total miles, and 40 percent of the transport-related emissions, in the food supply chain as a whole. That's because there are also "upstream" miles and emissions associated with things like transport of fertilizer, pesticides, and animal feed. Overall, transport accounts for about 11 percent of the food system's emissions. By contrast, Weber and Matthews found agricultural production accounts for the bulk of the food system's greenhouse gas emissions: 83 percent of emissions occur before food even leaves the farm gate. A recent life cycle analysis of the UK [United Kingdom] food system, by Tara Garnett, yielded similar results. In her study, transport accounted for about a tenth of the food system's greenhouse gas emissions, and agricultural production accounted for half. Garnett says the same general patterns likely also hold for Europe as a whole.

The Environmental Cost of What We Eat

The other clear result that emerges from these analyses is that what you eat matters at least as much as how far it travels, and agriculture's overwhelming "hot spots" are red meat and dairy production. In part that's due to the inefficiency of eating higher up on the food chain—it takes more energy, and generates more emissions, to grow grain, feed it to cows, and produce meat or dairy products for human consumption, than to feed grain to humans directly. But a large portion of emissions associated with meat and dairy production take the form of methane and nitrous oxide, greenhouse gases that are respectively 23 and 296 times as potent as carbon dioxide. Methane is produced by ruminant animals (cows, goats, sheep, and the like) as a by-product of digestion and is also released by the breakdown of all types of animal manure. Nitrous oxide also comes from the breakdown of manure (as well as the production and breakdown of fertilizers).

In Garnett's study, meat and dairy accounted for half of the UK food system's greenhouse gas emissions. In fact, she writes, "the major contribution made by agriculture itself reflects the GHG [greenhouse gas] intensity of livestock rearing." Weber and Matthews came to a similar conclusion: "No matter how it is measured, on average red meat is more GHG-intensive than all other forms of food," responsible for about 150 percent more emissions than chicken or fish. In their study the second-largest contributor to emissions was the dairy industry.

Nor are these two studies unique in their findings. A group of Swedish researchers has calculated that meat and dairy contribute 58 percent of the total food emissions from a typical Swedish diet. At a global level, the UN [United Nations] Food and Agriculture Organization has estimated that livestock account for 18 percent of all greenhouse gas emissions—more even than all forms of fossil fuel-based transport combined.

Replacing red meat and dairy with vegetables one day a week would be like driving 1,160 miles less.

Dietary Changes Are More Important Than Local Eating

"Broadly speaking, eating fewer meat and dairy products and consuming more plant foods in their place is probably the single most helpful behavioral shift one can make" to reduce food-related greenhouse gas emissions, Garnett argues.

Weber and Matthews calculated that reducing food miles to zero—an all-but-impossible goal in practice—would reduce the greenhouse gas emissions associated with the food system by only about 5 percent, equivalent to driving 1,000 miles less over the course of a year. By comparison, replacing red meat and dairy with chicken, fish, or eggs for one day per week would save the equivalent of driving 760 miles per year. Replacing red meat and dairy with vegetables one day a week would be like driving 1,160 miles less. "Thus," they write, "we suggest that dietary shift can be a more effective means of lowering an average household's food-related climate footprint than 'buying local.'"

However, Weber acknowledges, "these calculations were done assuming that local foods are no different than non-local foods." And that's not always the case. For example, local food advocates also emphasize eating seasonal (often meaning field-grown) and less processed foods. Those qualities, along with shorter distances from farm to table, will also contribute to lower emissions compared to the "average" diet.

The Benefits of Organic and Sustainable Farming

Food marketed in the local food economy—at farmers' markets and through community supported agriculture (CSA) schemes—is frequently also organic. Organic food often (though not always) is associated with lower greenhouse gas emissions than conventionally grown food, because organics don't generate the emissions associated with production, transport, and application of synthetic fertilizers and pesticides.

Organic food also has other environmental benefits; less use of toxic chemicals promotes greater farmland biodiversity, and organic fields require less irrigation under some conditions. Because local food is so frequently talked about in terms of food miles, its environmental benefits have largely been couched in terms of greenhouse gas emissions. But food's carbon footprint "can't be the only measuring stick of environmental sustainability," notes Gail Feenstra, a food systems analyst at the University of California, Davis's Sustainable Agriculture Research and Education program.

Finally, farmers who market locally are often relatively small in scale and can more feasibly adopt environmentally beneficial practices such as growing a diversity of crops, planting cover crops, leaving weedy field borders or planting hedgerows that provide a refuge for native biodiversity, and integrating crop and livestock production. In short, Weber says, "the production practices matter a lot more than where the food was actually grown. If buying local also means buying with better production practices then that's great, that's going to make a huge difference."

Of course, the relationship between local food marketing and sustainable agricultural practices is far from perfect. A small farmer can still spray pesticides and plow from road to road. Not all farmers' market vendors are organic. Clare Hinrichs, who calls herself an "ardent" farmers' market shopper, nevertheless acknowledges that "the actual consequences—both intended or unintended—[of local food systems] haven't really been all that closely or systematically studied."

Organic food also has other environmental benefits; less use of toxic chemicals promotes greater farmland biodiversity, and organic fields require less irrigation under some conditions.

The Farmer and Consumer Relationship

So, is local food greener? Not necessarily. But look at the question from the opposite direction: If you're a consumer interested in greener food, the local food economy is currently a good place to find it. By the same token, a farmer who sells in the local food economy might be more likely to adopt or continue sustainable practices in order to meet this customer demand. If local food has environmental benefits, they aren't all—or perhaps even mainly—intrinsic to localness. Or, as Hinrichs has written, "it is the social relation, not the spatial location, per se, that accounts for this outcome."

For local food advocates like Sage Van Wing, that interaction between producer and consumer, between farmer and eater, is precisely the point. Regarding food miles, Van Wing says, "I'm not interested in that at all." For her, purchasing an apple isn't about the greenhouse gas emissions involved in producing and transporting the fruit, "it's also about how those apples were farmed, how the farm workers were treated"—a broad array of ecological, social, and economic factors that add up to sustainability. Interacting directly with the farmer who grows her food creates a "standard of trust," she says.

Christopher Weber, who followed a vegan diet for ten years and calls himself "somewhat of a self-proclaimed foodie," agrees: "That's one thing that's really great about local food, and one of the reasons that I buy locally, is because you can actually know your farmer and know what they're doing."

Van Wing says that her approach to local food has evolved over time—she started out trying to eat within a 100-mile radius, but now she simply tries to get each food item from the closest source feasible. Foods that can't be grown nearby are either rare treats or have disappeared from her diet altogether. "I just don't do things that don't make sense," she says. Her statement echoes journalist and sustainable-agriculture guru Michael Pollan, who in his recent book *In Defense of Food: An Eater's Manifesto* offers a commonsense guide to eating ethically and well: "Eat food. Not too much. Mostly plants." You could sum up the ecological case for eating locally by adding one more sentence: "Mostly what's in season and grown not too far away."

Additional Considerations to Local Eating

Yet there are limits to this commonsense approach. In many areas, the climate is such that eating local, seasonal, field-grown produce would be a pretty bleak proposition for much of the year. Large concentrations of people live in areas not suited to growing certain staple crops; it's one thing to forego bananas, but quite another to give up wheat. And population density itself works against re-localization of the food system. Most of the land within 100 miles of large cities such as New York is itself very built up; where will the farmland to feed us all locally come from? (By the same token, that very situation makes preservation of what farmland remains all the more important, a goal that buying from local farmers can help advance.)

What if a greater investment in rail infrastructure helped to reverse the trend toward transporting more food by inefficient semitrucks?

In this sense, life cycle analyses of the current food system offer a paradoxically hopeful perspective, because they suggest that, if the goal is to improve the environmental sustainability of the food system as a whole, then there are a variety of public policy levers that we can pull. To be sure, promoting more localized food production and distribution networks would reduce transport emissions. But what if a greater investment in rail infrastructure helped to reverse the trend toward transporting more food by inefficient semitrucks? What if fuel economy standards were increased for the truck fleet that moves our food? Or, to name one encompassing possibility, what if a carbon-pricing system incorporated some of the environmental costs of agriculture that are currently externalized? Local food is delicious, but the problem—and perhaps the solution—is global.

8

Food Production Causes More Environmental Damage Than Food Miles

Robin McKie

Robin McKie is the science and technology editor for the Observer, *Britain's oldest Sunday newspaper.*

When people focus on food miles to make ethical shopping decisions, they are missing the big picture. Although these consumers often switch to local diets to reduce their carbon footprints, local foods often carry larger carbon footprints than their freighted counterparts. Farming methods, including pesticide use, and the type of food being produced, particularly animal products, as well as food storage and preparation methods can have a bigger impact on the environment than food miles. Additionally, the treatment of workers and the economic benefits to local communities, such as coffee growers in developing nations, should also be considered when making ethical purchases.

Mike Small and his wife, Karen, sat down last Thursday [March 2008] to a dinner of smoked fish pie crusted with mashed potatoes and served with purple-sprouting broccoli, an unremarkable family meal except for one key factor: Every ingredient came from sources close to their home in Burntisland, Fife [Scotland]. 'The fish was Fife-landed, while the potatoes and broccoli were grown on nearby farms,' he says.

The Local Diet

Nor was this a one-off culinary event. For the past six months Mike and Karen and their two children, Sorley and Alex, have consumed only food and drink bought in their home district.

This is the Fife Diet, developed by Mike Small as a response to the environmental dangers posed by carbon-emitting imports of Peruvian avocados, Kenyan green beans, New Zealand lamb and all those other foreign foodstuffs that now fill the shelves of our supermarkets. Each of these imported products involves the emission of carbon dioxide from the planes and ships that brought them to our shores.

So Mike Small argues that we should eat local produce and save the planet, an idea that has obliged his family—and a growing number of adherents to his cause—to eat meals of local lamb, pork and a great many dishes based on parsnips, beetroots, kale, potatoes, leeks and all the other root vegetables that typify the agricultural output of this windswept corner of Scotland.

The concept of food miles is unhelpful and stupid. It doesn't inform about anything except the distance travelled.

This is the future of ethical eating, insists Small: the consumption of local produce at all costs. It is an attitude now shared by thousands around the UK [United Kingdom] and overseas, individuals who have decided to reject foods that have been transported over long distances by road, air or sea to their dinner plates. They even have their own name for themselves—locavores—and insist that their way is the only one to save the planet.

The Problem with Food Miles

But the idea that 'only local is good' has come under attack. For a start, food grown in areas where there is high use of fertilisers and tractors is likely to be anything but carbon friendly, it is pointed out. At the same time the argument against food miles—which show how far a product has been shipped and therefore how much carbon has been emitted in its transport—has been savaged by experts. 'The concept of food miles is unhelpful and stupid. It doesn't inform about anything except the distance travelled,' Dr Adrian Williams, of the National Resources Management Centre at Cranfield University, told the *Observer* last week.

Given that the food miles cause was hailed only a few months ago as the means to empower the carbon-conscious consumer, such criticisms are striking, and suggest that some careful reassessment of the concept's usefulness has been going on.

Calculating Carbon Emissions

Certainly the issues involved no longer seem clear-cut. Consider that supermarket stalwart: green beans from Kenya. These are airfreighted to stores to allow consumers to buy fresh beans when British varieties are out of season. Each packet has a little sticker with the image of a plane on it to indicate that carbon dioxide from aviation fuel was emitted in bringing them to this country. And that, surely, is bad, campaigners argue. Rising levels of carbon dioxide are trapping more and more sunlight and inexorably heating the planet, after all.

Driving 6.5 miles to buy your shopping emits more carbon than flying a pack of Kenyan green beans to the UK.

But a warning that beans have been airfreighted does not mean we should automatically switch to British varieties if we want to help the climate. Beans in Kenya are produced in a highly environmentally friendly manner. 'Beans there are grown using manual labour—nothing is mechanised,' says

Professor Gareth Edwards-Jones of Bangor University, an expert on African agriculture. 'They don't use tractors, they use cow muck as fertiliser; and they have low-tech irrigation systems in Kenya. They also provide employment to many people in the developing world. So you have to weigh that against the air miles used to get them to the supermarket.'

Local Is Not Always Better

When you do that—and incorporate these different factors—you make the counterintuitive discovery that air-transported green beans from Kenya could actually account for the emission of less carbon dioxide than British beans. The latter are grown in fields on which oil-based fertilisers have been sprayed and which are ploughed by tractors that burn diesel. In the words of Gareth Thomas, Minister for Trade and Development, speaking at a recent Department for International Development airfreight seminar: 'Driving 6.5 miles to buy your shopping emits more carbon than flying a pack of Kenyan green beans to the UK.'

'Half the people who boycott airfreighted beans think they are doing some good for the environment. Then they go on a budget airline holiday to Prague the next weekend,' adds Bill Vorley, head of sustainable markets for the International Institute for Environment and Development. 'They are just making gestures.'

Two Complex Examples

It is not that the concept of food miles is wrong; it is just too simplistic, say experts. In fact, balancing your diet with its carbon costs turns out to be a fiendishly tricky business. Consider these two staples: apples and lettuce. The former are harvested in September and October. Some are sold fresh; the rest are chill-stored. For most of the following year, they still represent good value—in terms of carbon emissions—for British shoppers. But by August those Cox's [apples] and Braeburns will have been in stores for 10 months. The amount of energy used to keep them fresh for that length of time will then overtake the carbon cost of shipping them from New Zealand. It is therefore better for the environment if UK shoppers buy apples from New Zealand in July and August rather than those of British origin.

Then there is the example of lettuces. In Britain these are grown in winter, in greenhouses or polytunnels, which require heating. At those times it is better—in terms of carbon emissions—to buy field-grown lettuce from Spain. But in summer, when no heating is required, British is best. Picking the right sources for your apples and lettuces depends on the time of year.

'Working out carbon footprints is horribly complicated,' says Edwards-Jones. 'It is not just where something is grown and how far it has to travel, but also how it is grown, how it is stored, how it is prepared.'

It is not that the concept of food miles is wrong; it is just too simplistic.

Organic vs. Local

This uncertainty even extends to the Soil Association [an organic campaigning and certification body] which announced last year that it was considering halting its endorsement of airfreighted organic food because their emissions negated the benefits of growing it organically. But now the organisation has dropped the plan and is to continue to endorse airfreighted organic food, provided it is grown under conditions that meet its ethical trade standards.

In addition, the government has revealed that it is changing its stance on food miles, as was recently stressed by Gareth Thomas. 'Food miles alone are not the best way to judge whether the food we eat is sustainable. We need a better-informed food miles debate. Long term, the only fair option is to ensure the prices of the goods we consume, including organic produce, cover the environmental costs wherever the goods are from. We also need a labelling system that tells consumers about how the product is reducing poverty.'

Supermarkets and Manufacturers React

Nor is this argument lost on the nation's supermarkets. 'An airplane sticker is of no environmental value whatsoever, as studies have shown airfreighted products are not necessarily less sustainable than local produce grown in heated greenhouses,' said a spokesman for Tesco [a UK-based grocery chain]. 'Thus we may remove those plane labels in the future. What people are actually interested in is the amount of carbon that is emitted during a product's manufacture and import.' As a result, Tesco has promised to put carbon labels on 30 of its own brand products in the near future: six types of potatoes, 11 types of tomatoes, five types of washing power and liquid capsules, four types of orange juice and six types of lightbulbs. 'We want to see how customers react and find out how it affects their purchasing behaviour,' added the spokesman.

In fact, these carbon-cost labels have already been tested on a small range of products, including Walkers' crisps [potato chips] and Cadbury's chocolates. Packets and wrappers have a small C with a downward arrow through it, beside a figure which represents the number of grams of carbon dioxide emitted during the manufacture of that product. In this way it is revealed that packets of Walkers' ready salted and salt and vinegar crisps each generate 75g [grams] of carbon, while the cheese and onion variety produced only 74g.

Now this limited range of products is to be expanded and will appear in Tesco and other stores, says the Carbon Trust, which—with the British Standards Institution—has been involved in calculating how a meaningful carbon inventory can be compiled for foodstuffs.

Creating Carbon-Cost Labels

Not surprisingly, such exercises have proved to be extraordinarily tricky, says Graham Sinden of the Carbon Trust. 'You have to take into account emissions that occurred in the farmyard, for example. Cows and sheep produce methane, which is far more damaging a greenhouse gas than carbon dioxide. Similarly, fertilisers produce nitrogen oxides that are also dangerous. Then you have the issue of transport and processing. Taking a sheep to the slaughterhouse produces carbon emissions, for instance. Cooking is another factor. That requires heat that in turn releases carbon dioxide. After that you need to store products. That often requires refrigeration, which requires electricity, which releases carbon dioxide. Estimating how long a product will be kept in a store and how efficient is its refrigeration is not easy to assess, but it has to be done.

How can you accurately calculate a pizza's carbon footprint when it often comes with a variety of toppings?

'Then you have to work out how long your product will be kept at home once it has been purchased. You also have to estimate how efficiently it will be cooked. And finally you have to work out how much carbon is involved in its packaging and how much will be emitted in disposing of those wrappers and labels once discarded.'

For some products, such as crisps, a carbon number is easy to calculate. But for others, the process will be much more awkward. How can you accurately calculate a pizza's carbon footprint when it often comes with a variety of toppings?

Other Factors to Consider in Ethical Eating

Even if you could get a carbon label that accurately reflects a product's impact on the environment and identify products that have high footprints, would you be right in boycotting them? In many cases, such as brands of coffee, these products come from struggling third world nations. Using our Western concerns with the climate as an excuse to increase poverty there has dubious ethical consequences.

There is only one way of being sure that you cut down on your carbon emissions when buying food: Stop eating meat, milk, butter and cheese.

In short, the issue of trying to reduce the emissions produced by food is bedeviled by complexity. Even replacing food miles with a carbon footprint figure will only partly simplify the issues, a point stressed by Tara Garnett of the Food Climate Research Network.

'There is only one way of being sure that you cut down on your carbon emissions when buying food: Stop eating meat, milk, butter and cheese,' said Garnett. 'These come from ruminants—sheep and cattle—that produce a great deal of harmful methane. In other words, it is not the source of the food that matters, but the kind of food you eat. Whether people are prepared to cut these from their shopping lists is a different issue, however.'

Chickpeas: An Example

Chickpeas are sold in supermarkets in two versions: dried or cooked. The carbon footprint of the latter is far higher than the former. The only processing involved in drying chickpeas is to lay them out in the sun to drive off moisture. By contrast, heat is needed to cook chickpeas before they are tinned. Hence the carbon gram total for tins of cooked chickpeas would be far greater than those on packets of the dried variety.

'That seems straightforward,' says Graham Sinden, of the Carbon Trust. 'But you can't eat dried chickpeas. You have to cook them. And when you take them home you find the carbon you emitted when cooking those chickpeas exceeds the figure for the tinned variety—because cooking small portions at home is inefficient compared with that of large industrial kitchens.'

As a result, when the trust system is taken up and used widely, the gram measure on a packet of dried chickpeas will include an estimate of the heat that will be used in a customer's home to cook them. But that figure will be a guess, for it will depend on whether the customer uses gas or electricity for cooking. The former is more efficient and less prone to carbon emissions.

As for individuals who use renewable energy to heat their homes and kitchens, they would completely negate the point of carbon labels in many cases. 'That is why it is impossible to have accurate carbon labels on a lot of products,' says Gareth Edwards-Jones, of Bangor University.

9

Buying Local Is Good for the Consumer, the Farmer, and the Planet

Brian Halweil

Brian Halweil is a senior researcher with the Worldwatch Institute and the author of several articles and the book Home Grown: The Case for Local Food in a Global Market.

The popularity of local foods is increasing rapidly with consumers, and grassroots movements are springing up around the country to bring local foods into schools and even prisons. Meanwhile, restaurants are following suit, incorporating seasonal eating into their menus to make use of the local food supply. There are many reasons to eat local, but consumers frequently make the choice to consume local foods simply to have more control over what they eat. In addition to seeking farming practices that reduce pesticide and antibiotics use and ensure the fair working conditions of farm workers, consumers also seek out local foods to buy the freshest, tastiest foods possible.

My wife and I live in an old whaling town on the eastern end of Long Island, New York, where we tend a home garden and orchard. For much of the year, we don't have to buy produce. In the winter, we eat what we've canned, pickled, dried, and otherwise put up. We get eggs from a neighbor, trading him vegetables. We rake our own oysters and clams. We have a few local bakers who turn out warm, crusty loaves

Brian Halweil, "Food Revolution: Americans Lose Their Appetite for Anonymous Food," *Yes! Magazine*, February 19, 2006. Reproduced by permission of the author.

each day, and a cheese shop that offers dozens of American farmstead cheeses—including a few made from the milk of cows grazing a few miles away.

Reasons for Eating Local

Of course, there's still room on our table for exotic flavors, including coffee, chocolate, and other imported pleasures. But eating this way means that we don't get strawberries in the winter or wild salmon from Alaska or many other things that aren't in season or aren't from here. Which we don't mind much, since we always know exactly what we're putting in our mouths.

The more I've come to rely on local food, the more I see why so many Americans are hungry for alternatives to the corporate supermarket.

The farther removed we are from where our food is raised, the less we know about it.

Walk through the sliding glass doors and you find brightly colored cereal boxes, mounds of vegetables, an entire frigid wall of dairy products and frozen dinners.

But what you don't see is information about how or where the food was raised. Our food travels farther than ever before—at least 1,500 miles for the average item in the United States. The farther removed we are from where our food is raised, the less we know about it. None of the cryptic nutritional labels will mention that some of the seafood contains mercury and other heavy metals, that the strawberries may have been misted with chemicals banned in much of the rest of the world, that the milk you are buying for your kids may contain traces of hormones fed to the cows to make them produce more milk. No label describes the working conditions for farmers or farm workers.

The Growing Popularity of Local Eating

More and more Americans are fed up with this sort of anonymous food. In the last decade, a veritable cornucopia of choices has become available that now allows us to take greater control of the food supply.

In the last ten years, interest in eating local has exploded, whether you count the growth in farmers' markets (roughly 3,800 nationwide, more than twice the number a decade ago); membership in Slow Food USA (13,000 members and 145 chapters just since 2000), the American arm of an international movement to defend our collective "right to taste" as well as the artisanal food producers who bring us distinctive flavors; or the number of schools stocking their cafeterias with fresh food raised by nearby farmers (400 school districts in 22 states, in addition to dozens of colleges and universities).

Grassroots Movements

YES! has documented the inspiring grassroots movement referred to by parents, farmers, and teachers as "farm to school" that is sweeping the nation, as well as many other examples of communities declaring independence from the standard food chain. There's the story of Anna Marie Carter, "The Seed Lady of Watts," a master gardener who uses organic farming to improve the lives of people suffering from illness or poverty, or the People's Grocery in West Oakland [California], founded to get city kids involved in growing and selling fresh fruits and veggies in a neighborhood sorely in need of such sustenance, or the many jails around the nation where inmates use gardening as therapy.

Within the food landscape, the fastest-growing category remains organic food, sales of which have been increasing at nearly 20 percent each year for the last decade, eight times faster than the relatively stagnant grocery sector as a whole. Organic food sales topped $10 billion in 2003 and are expected to hit $32.3 billion by 2009, as top supermarkets and food conglomerates roll out their own private-label organic foods. (Although such popularity means more acres farmed without polluting pesticides and chemical fertilizers, it has raised concerns about attempts to water down organic standards in the name of profit.)

More Reasons to Eat Local Foods

Even some large and influential agribusiness companies are beginning to declare some allegiance to place. "We've been pleasantly surprised by how easy it has been for our chefs to create these menus," said Maisie Ganzler, director of communications and strategic initiatives for Palo Alto-based Bon Appétit Management Company, a food service industry pioneer in serving food from sustainable, local sources. The company's Eat Local challenge in September of 2005 galvanized 190 cafés, restaurants, and university eateries owned by the company to serve at least one meal made only from ingredients grown within a 150-mile radius. "We were motivated by flavor," said Ganzler, who noted that the company will expand their local offerings based on the challenge's success: "Once you taste the difference in the food, it's very hard to go back."

The closer you are to where your food is raised the more power you have over how it is raised.

Yes, eating local does taste better. It also saves huge amounts of oil, keeps money in your local economy, and combats sprawl by keeping land outside cities and towns in farmers' hands. It even pleases the Department of Homeland Security, because shipping less food makes our nation less vulnerable to disruption of the transportation system, to spikes in oil prices, or to large-scale food contamination.

It also means peace of mind, because the closer you are to where your food is raised the more power you have over how it is raised.

Maintaining Control over Your Diet

Eating local is the easiest way to eliminate suspect food from your diet. It's also the easiest way to cut processed foods with added fat and sugar out of your diet, since you'll be buying more fresh fruits and vegetables.

In a small but significant way, Americans who choose to buy their food from nearby farmers, fishers, and food makers are making a sort of declaration of independence. The ranks of the rebels include parents, fed up with what their children are served at school, who get fresh produce into the cafeteria; farmers holding on to their livelihoods by selling to nearby restaurants; and city politicians who make space for farmers' markets, community gardens, and urban farms. They include people who are buying as much organic produce, range-fed meat, sustainable seafood, and fair trade coffee as is available.

It's not always easy to eat this way. It means being less impressed by flashy packaging or volume discounts and more inclined to be curious and vigilant. But it always leaves a better taste in your mouth.

10

The Distance Food Travels Is Damaging to the Environment

Marc Xuereb

Marc Xuereb is a public health planner with the Region of Waterloo Public Health, where he authored the frequently cited study "Food Miles: Environmental Implication of Food Imports to Waterloo Region," which documents the distance and greenhouse gas emissions associated with food transport.

Three separate Canadian studies, using different methods, recently offered an alarming, though consistent, look at the environmental cost of imported foods. The results from these studies challenged earlier findings and showed greenhouse gas emissions from food miles are even higher than previously thought. However, a solution to reducing these greenhouse gases with local eating is within reach. Consumers can make a big impact by choosing locally grown foods, and with only small changes, local farmers can produce enough food locally to provide consumers with everything they need to meet Canada's Food Guide requirements.

If the veggies on your plate look a little tired, don't be surprised. They likely travelled a long way before landing on your table, farther than you might think. Three recent Canadian studies have documented the distances that typical foods travel and the findings are staggering.

Now, in addition to the economic and social arguments for rebuilding local "food sheds," we have Canadian "food

Marc Xuereb, "And Miles to Go Before I Eat. Home-Grown Hurrah," *Alternatives Journal*, vol. 32, August 1, 2006, pp. 18–19.

miles" data. They strengthen arguments for local food policy initiatives. I was involved in producing the most recent of three Canadian studies, which the Region of Waterloo Public Health published in 2005. The others were completed by Victoria's LifeCycles Project Society and by Toronto's Food-Share in 2004. In combination, these studies make a powerful statement about our food systems.

Calculating the Distance Food Travels

Before the release of these reports, Canadian activists depended on "Food, Fuel, and Freeways," a study conducted in 2001 by Iowa's Leopold Center for Sustainable Agriculture. It determined that food passing through a Chicago food terminal had traveled an average distance of 1,500 miles (2,400 km [kilometres]) before getting to destinations in Iowa.

The Canadian studies were unable to replicate the methodology of the Leopold study due to differences in the availability of Canadian food transport data, so a direct comparison isn't possible. However, while the Canadian studies differ from one another, they all compare foods that can be grown locally—tomatoes, cheese, oats, chicken and yogurt, for example—with those that cannot—bananas, oranges and rice, for instance. As a result, they offer a consistent comparison between the environmental costs of local versus imported foods.

Three Approaches to Determining Food Miles

FoodShare took the most straightforward and replicable approach. Its authors selected a typical dinner menu and then shopped for the ingredients at a Toronto farmers' market and at a supermarket. Tracing the foods' origins using product labels, they compared food miles and found that the supermarket foods traveled, on average, 81 times farther than the farmers' market foods. Then, using assumptions about the travel modes of the imported foods, they calculated greenhouse gas (GHG) emissions resulting from their transport and concluded that a year of choosing local over imported would save half a tonne of GHG emissions per household.

The LifeCycles project in Victoria used Statistics Canada data to calculate average travel distances for all imports of dozens of foods. It then made similar travel mode assumptions to calculate GHG emissions for imports of each. The data are easily accessible on the LifeCycles Web site, where one can quickly find average import distances for a wide range of foods and then switch to a database of local producers of the same foods. For example, cheese imports have a high level of GHG emissions, travelling over 13,000 km on average from places like New Zealand and Europe, while Vancouver Island residents can find local yogurt from at least 10 farms listed on the LifeCyles Web site.

The Waterloo Region study followed the LifeCyles approach, but did not link the findings to a database of local producers, nor did it put the findings on a Web-based database. Instead, it added two unique features of its own: a calculation of the average food miles and GHG emissions for all the studied foods, and a calculation of the total environmental cost of the region's consumption of the imported foods.

Beef travelled an average of 5,770 kilometres and produced five times its weight in GHG emissions.

The Waterloo Region Results

The study found that 58 imported foods travel almost 4,500 kilometres on average, creating more than their own weight in GHG emissions during transportation. Imports of the studied foods account for 51,709 tonnes of GHG emissions annually in Waterloo Region. This is equivalent to over a quarter tonne per household, or over 16,000 cars on the road. Amazingly, however, 99 percent of the annual GHG emissions could be eliminated if the studied foods were replaced with local ones, assuming they traveled 30 kilometres. Increase this distance to 250 kilometres and GHG emission reductions still added up to a 96-percent saving.

Beef imports were the Waterloo study's most extreme example. Beef travelled an average of 5,770 kilometres and produced five times its weight in GHG emissions. These data are particularly perplexing since the Waterloo area is well known for its beef farms. Driving the figures upward is the large number of imports from distant Australia and New Zealand. Together, they accounted for 27 percent of all beef imports to the region.

Is Eating Local Possible?

A separate Region of Waterloo Public Health analysis addressed the practicality of replacing imported foods with local ones. Released in 2005, the "Optimal Nutrition Environment [for Waterloo Region, 2006–2046]" study found that production of the foods necessary to provide residents with a diet that satisfied Canada's Food Guide required a shift in production on only 10 to 12 percent of local agricultural lands. In other words, if some Waterloo Region farmers who currently grow products that local residents already get enough of (e.g., feed for livestock, corn or soy) were to switch to growing foods not currently available in sufficient quantities (e.g., fruits, vegetables and whole grains), the population could sustain itself from local lands.

It may not be possible for many regions of Canada to grow as much of their own food as Waterloo Region. This area includes three mid-sized cities (Cambridge, Kitchener and Waterloo) as well as four rural townships and boasts some of the most productive farms in Ontario. But, as we have seen, even replacing imports with food from several counties away can make a huge difference.

11

Follow That French Fry: Food Miles and Roadway Damage

Gretchen Stoeltje

Gretchen Stoeltje is a researcher in the Government and Public Affairs Division of the Texas Department of Transportation.

Consumers may have the power to relieve stress on our overburdened highway system, provide a boost to local economies, and reduce air pollution simply by making different choices at the market. State governments would be wise to support the growing local food movement and help educate consumers about the real cost of imported food to help their state economies, reduce pollution, and save the crumbling roadways. Consumers can be educated through food labels that indicate the distance items traveled to the supermarket as well as by explaining to them what can be grown locally and the benefits of buying local. For example, local and imported fresh foods travel far less than processed foods, and farmers receive a greater share of the profit when foods are purchased locally rather than sold for export. Once consumers understand the real costs associated with imported foods, their choices are likely to reflect those facts.

How Much Road Do We Chew Up When We Eat?

See that shiny, red apple on your table? Do you know what it costs? You may know what you paid for it at the store, but the full cost of transporting a simple piece of fruit from the or-

Gretchen Stoeltje, *Follow That French Fry: Food Miles and Roadway Damage*, Policy Research Paper, TX: Texas Department of Transportation, 2008. Government & Public Affairs Division, Policy Research Paper, March 25, 2008 from pages 2–12. Reproduced by permission.

chard to your home includes other intangibles not reflected in the retail price, like the distance food travels and the external costs of that journey. Food miles is the name of a new set of metrics designed to measure—and potentially help us manage—the impact of those intangibles. Recently, thanks to a spate of news stories about global warming and tainted food products from China, consumers and others are starting to ask questions about the real costs of common foods. Parents, health officials, and anyone anxious to avoid unsafe food are concerned about contaminated imports and the government's inability to track them. Environmentalists concerned about the emissions levels from long-distance food transport have raised questions about their impact on air quality. Even major investment bankers convinced that we have exhausted our oil supplies warn that we must abandon our oil-dependent food transport system. The transportation sector, and the taxpayers who pay for it, have not yet started asking tough questions about the real costs of food transport. But with growing concerns about our decaying interstates—and the long, hard miles traveled by staples such as french fries, fruits and grains—it's time we start.

Consider: Most food in the United States travels a very long way from its point of origin to its point of consumption—some 1,500 miles, on average[1]—typically in trucks that can each cause the same amount of roadway damage as 9,600 cars.[2] But a recent Iowa study found that foods grown in-state only traveled 56 miles from Iowa farmer to Iowa consumer.[3] Are all these extra miles necessary? What is their true cost? And what can we eat or not eat to reduce the demand for, and damage to, our roads? At another time and place, these questions might not seem so pressing. But today, we are in the midst of an escalating national mobility crisis. The Highway Trust Fund is set to run dry in 2009;[4] Congress and most states have declined to raise the gas tax since the early 1990s;[5] and our transportation network is falling apart.[6] If the need for infrastructure maintenance wasn't glaringly apparent before, the collapse of the I-35W bridge in Minneapolis last summer should have brought it into clear focus. According to the National Conference of State Legislatures, we are facing a transportation funding gap which, by 2015, could be as wide as $1,000,000,000,000 (1 trillion dollars).[7] Given this alarming state of affairs, policy makers and consumers alike might want to consider innovative solutions, like the evaluation and management of food miles that can help us preserve our nation's aging roadways.

Do the Math: What's in a Food Mile?

Food miles researchers measure the external costs, or externalities, of long-distance food transport. Externalities are the costs of a process borne by society as a whole and not borne by the transport user or operator.[8] Roadway wear and tear is one example of a food transport externality. Others include congestion, carbon emissions, compromised roadway safety, and ailing local agricultural economies. A food miles study can measure these external costs, driven by such pointed questions as: How much congestion could we reduce? How much time and money could we save? How much could we reduce polluting emissions? How much economic opportunity could we create? What might we lose? And what might we gain by changing our food transport system?

Researchers in England, Canada, and Iowa, have asked and answered some of these questions in recent food miles studies. In Britain, the amount of food moved by Heavy Goods Vehicles (HGVs) has increased 23% since 1978 so that food transport now constitutes 25% of HGV traffic in the UK, costing over £9 billion each year in congestion-dominated environmental, social and economic costs.[9] The Department of the Environment, Food and Rural Affairs (Defra) measured food transport's share of congestion, infrastructure damage, accidents, carbon dioxide emissions, bad air quality, and noise and found that a combination of six different solutions could result in a 17.3% reduction in the cost of domestic food transport externalities.[10]

Canadian researchers at the Region of Waterloo Public Health Department in Ontario measured the distances traveled by imported food, all of which could be grown or raised in the Waterloo Region, as well as the greenhouse gas emissions resulting from the transport of this imported food. The results showed that replacing the studied food items with locally produced equivalents would annually reduce greenhouse gas emissions by 49,485 metric tonnes, the equivalent of taking 16,191 cars off the roads.[11]

And in the US, the Leopold Center for Sustainable Agriculture at Iowa State University has produced several studies measuring a number of different external costs. In one, researchers examined three levels of food transportation systems: the conventional system using large semitrailer trucks; Iowa-based regional systems, using large semitrailer and mid-size trucks; and local systems, using small light trucks. This study found that conventionally sourced and transported food in the United States traveled 1,518 miles to reach the table in 1998, a 22% increase since 1981.[12] In July 2003 a second Leopold Center study of food miles compared the distance that 16 different produce items traveled to an institutional market, both when grown close to home, and when grown elsewhere in the United States and transported to Iowa conventionally. The locally grown food traveled an average of 56 miles (between 20 and 75), while conventionally sourced food traveled an average of 1,494 miles (between 311 and 1,838) before they reached market.[13]

These studies offer compelling evidence that reducing even some of our food miles is not only possible but possibly beneficial to congestion relief, air quality improvement and roadway safety enhancement efforts. What most food miles studies did not calculate—but that other researchers could—is the number of roadway miles that would be preserved by reducing conventional food transport or the amount of roadway that could be funded and maintained by charging consumers the true cost to transport their food.

You Mean My Roads Aren't Immortal?

Transportation systems, especially roads, are easily taken for granted because they seem so permanent, and they always seem to work—until one day, they just don't. Americans have rarely been forced to collectively recognize the mortality of our roads because we only began building them, on a national scale in 1956.[14] So we are only now learning what happens when aging transportation systems begin to fail and what it costs to replace them. Roadway maintenance in the US, like new construction, is a hidden but nevertheless real cost that citizens pay in part when they purchase gasoline or pay a vehicle registration fee, but never see itemized on any bill. Not so hard to see are the costs the traveling public pays for ailing roads in the form of increased car care. A 2008 report by TRIP, a Washington D.C.-based, national transportation research group, found that the average American motorist pays an additional $413.00 annually for additional vehicle maintenance needs and increased fuel consumption caused by driving on poorly maintained roads.[15]

Food makes up a significant portion of roadway freight. In Texas alone, a 2006 measure of roadway freight showed that 26% of all trucks hauling freight to, from and within the state bore food.[16] The United States Department of Transportation expects that number to increase to 29% by the year 2035.[17] Moreover, these trucks do not pay their share of highway costs in proportion to the damage they cause. The Federal Highway Administration finds that cars typically pay their share of highway costs, and that pickups and vans typically pay more than their share of highway costs. But according to American Association of State Highway and Transit Officials, the extra weight borne by freight hauling vehicles, typically single-unit trucks and combination trucks, imposes the same amount of roadway damage as 9,600 cars,[18] yet those trucks only pay between 60% and 90% of their share of highway costs.[19] So from a transportation perspective, reducing the number of food-bearing trucks or funding those that continue to use our roads could start to look like serious roadway preservation.

Travels with Twinkie: Processed Food Miles

Processed foods are super globe-trotters and travel many more miles than fresh food. So roads take a greater beating from, say, a french fry than they do from a carrot. And though processed food may be cheaply priced and convenient, it may not merit the energy used to move it or our financial commitment to it. Eric Schlosser's best seller *Fast Food Nation*, revealed that Americans spend about 90% of their food budgets on processed foods.[20] However processed food, as opposed to fresh food, requires many more miles traveled in the processing than simply the distance between where it is grown and where it gets consumed. All of the separate components of any one processed food product must be manufactured and transported, and not always to or from the same locations. Schlosser's description of the life cycle of a typical potato used in the fast-food industry makes this point. Grown in Idaho, the potato will be transported from field to processing plant, perhaps in Idaho, perhaps not. There it will be sliced, diced and infused with chemically manufactured smells and flavors (produced in New Jersey), and preservatives, (so that it is safe and palatable after its many weeks-long journey from farm to fork), before being packaged and shipped to fast-food restaurants and grocery stores across the country as a frozen french fry.[21]

Some foods actually criss-cross the globe for processing or packaging before they return home for local sale. In the British Isles, for example, Scottish prawns are shipped to China to be hand-shelled, then shipped back to Scotland where they are breaded and then sold.[22] Haddock, caught by British trawlers in the Atlantic, goes to Poland for processing, and then back to Britain for sale.[23] Welsh cockles find their way to Holland to be pickled and canned before winding up on British supermarket shelves.[24] There is no doubt that, if packaged in Britain, British seafood would be more expensive because British labor is more expensive than Chinese or Dutch labor.[25] However, globe-trotting, cheap food isn't really cheap. We just don't see the full costs on food price tags because some of those costs we pay at the gas pump.

How Much Did That Burger Really Cost?

Lost Economic Opportunities

We also pay for cheap food in the form of economic loss to our local agricultural economy. "Get the Farmer Out of the Mud" was the slogan of the early nationwide push to get farm goods to market, known in Texas as the Farm to Market Road system.[26] In the early 20th century, rural Texas roads were often little more than deep, rutted trenches. Congress authorized the repair and upgrade of rural routes in 1912 enabling farmers to more easily transport and sell the fruits of their labor.[27] Today's food transport system begs this question, though: What farmers, and what markets? Economist John Ikerd estimates that American farmers, on average, make only about 20 cents of each food dollar spent; the remaining 80 cents going to pay for processing, transportation, packing and other marketing costs.[28] "Farmers who sell direct to local customers, on the other hand receive the full retail value, a dollar for each food dollar spent."[29] And for every dollar a food shopper spends on local food, the local food economy gains about three dollars.[30]

States have begun to plug the leaks in their agricultural economies. In August of 2007, the Illinois legislature enacted the Illinois Food, Farms and Jobs Act. The law provides for support of local and organic Illinois farming efforts in the hopes of keeping food dollars within the state, thereby revitalizing the Illinois state economy.[31] Among the findings that support the bill are the facts that food consumed in Illinois traveled 1,500 miles to the state's consumers, but that only 0.2% of Illinois farm sales comprised food sold directly for in state human consumption.[32]

In Texas, the Department of Agriculture's Go Texan program already promotes Texas grown-and-raised products, proudly announcing that Texas is the third largest agricultural commodities exporter in the nation. But while Texas sells live animals and red meat, wheat, and feeds and fodder to out of state buyers,[33] by fall 2007, only 11% of food available in Central Texas was grown locally. Furthermore, while Texas is the second largest agricultural state in the nation, it surpasses all of the other states in prime farmland loss and is therefore less and less able to feed its own population.[34] What would an increase in direct sales of locally grown food do for the Texas farmer and rancher? For the Texas economy?

Bad Air

Measuring the effects of food miles on air quality has been a tricky and often-challenged proposition. The reason is that, in some cases, it actually creates less air pollution overall to produce food sustainably in a remote part of the world and transport it to its point of consumption than it does to grow it locally. Sometimes growing that same food locally requires more energy. For example, one study found that growing a tomato in chilly Britain, out of season and under glass, requires more energy than growing it in sunny Spain and shipping it, by water, to Britain.[35] Therefore, it can be an oversimplification to say that sourcing food from remote locations is bad for air quality or for the environment in general.

Nevertheless, what can be said about the polluting emissions from conventional, roadway food transport is that reducing food miles would reduce the emissions of food-hauling trucks. Measuring those miles would show the potential amount of that reduction, as it has in previous studies. UK food miles studies showed that food transport produced 19 million tonnes (metric) of carbon dioxide in 2002.[36] Canadian researchers in Waterloo estimate that locally sourcing the foods they studied would result in an annual reduction of 49,485 tonnes of greenhouse gas emissions (metric).[37] And in Iowa, researchers at the Leopold Center found that locally sourcing just 10% more produce than the state currently does would result in a reduction of Iowa CO_2 emissions of 6.7 to 7.9 million pounds.[38] Iowa's potential reduction, estimated from only a 10% projected shift to local food production, accounts for .13% of total US CO_2 emissions from energy and industry for 2006 (6,045 million metric tons.)[39] If other states reduced conventional food transport by 10% or more, that number could increase significantly.

Congestion

"What causes congestion? In a word, you."[40]

While reducing congestion is the primary focus of state departments of transportation everywhere, actually changing this situation requires a movement that only travelers and freight consumers can truly launch, for they are its first cause.[41] According to the most recent findings from the Texas Transportation Institute, "The 2007 Urban Mobility Report," congestion is at an all-time high and getting "worse in urban areas of all sizes."[42] In Texas, for instance, metropolitan Texans lose up to 58 hours of their time to congestion annually and waste as much as 42 gallons of fuel each year.[43] Given these numbers, travelers and consumers should welcome any information that empowers them to change that situation. Commercial truck traffic makes up as much as 38% of traffic on Texas roadways.[44] Reducing even a small percent of truck travel related to food could have an impact.

Roadway Fatalities

Another reason to reduce truck traffic on regular roads is to improve safety. Roadway fatalities from crashes involving trucks reached 5,200 in 2005, and of those fatalities, only 803 were truck occupants.[45] The other 4,400 were occupants of lighter vehicles. Reducing the number of trucks on regular roads could save thousands of lives.

Hop That Train

Public interest in food sourcing has risen dramatically in recent years, and consumers are now more than ever shopping for local food. Farmers' markets, community supported agriculture programs, food circles, and institutional food programs that source locally are on the rise. Inspired by authors James McKinnon and Alisa Smith who, for one year ate food sourced from within a 100-mile radius of their home in Vancouver, communities across the country are taking up the 100 Mile Diet Challenge.[46] Restaurants everywhere feature menus that pull from the local food shed, and grocery stores not only sell, but label, locally sourced food. The food magazine franchise Edible Communities now serves 40 North American communities, publishing a seasonal, quarterly magazine named for the community it serves (for example, *Edible Austin*), and devoted entirely to that area's local food sources.[47] So prevalent is the phenomenon that the *New Oxford American Dictionary* declared *locavore*, or one who eats locally sourced food, the 2007 word of the year.[48] The issue even hit the cover of *Time* magazine in March of 2007, making it a trend, a craze, even a fashion. But first it is a demand.

A September 2007 study conducted by the Leopold Center for Sustainable Agriculture surveyed 500 consumers on how and where food is sourced, and the corresponding environmental impacts. The study concluded that consumer concerns about food safety, food sourcing, and the environmental impact and cost of the current food system have grown so quickly that the issue warrants a multi-agency investigation into our food supply chains.[49] The results are telling. Almost half of the respondents were willing to pay a 10% to 30% premium for food produced in a food supply chain that emitted half as much greenhouse gas as a conventional supply chain; 69% "somewhat" or "strongly" agreed that local food is healthier to eat than food that has traveled across the country; and 85% of respondents believed that local food is safe or somewhat safe, while only 12% could say the same for the global food system.[50] Accurate or not, consumer perceptions drive choice and demand.

With enough momentum, demands like this have brought about policy changes in ways that governmental regulation cannot. The organic food revolution, with its radical changes in food growing and consuming practices, is one such example. In his 2006 best seller, *The Omnivore's Dilemma*, Michael Pollan describes how pesticide-free farming, food co-ops, and a counterculture cuisine based on organic ingredients combined to create an informed consumer base that eventually demanded organic food. The result is an $11 billion organic marketplace, the product of "consumers and farmers working informally together outside the system, with exactly no help from the government."[51] *Fast Food Nation* author Eric Schlosser credits McDonald's customers with driving important health and safety changes in the meat packing industry that would have taken Congress years to achieve. Competition for customers between the major fast-food chains requires a quick responsiveness to consumer demand, and McDonald's consumers were demanding healthier food. In response McDonald's began pressuring their suppliers to deliver ground beef that was free of lethal pathogens. Suppliers increased investment in new equipment and microbial testing, and began producing a less toxic beef supply to all American consumers, not just McDonald's customers.[52]

If consumers do wield the power to make change, state governments might want to consider riding this wave of consumer interest in food sourcing by measuring those food miles and naming the implications. Clearly, some of these food miles are necessary since not all regions can grow food in equal measure. However, at this point in the transportation story, it is worth investigating all possibly extraneous food miles traveled. If we measure food miles, calculate the costs, and publicize results, people might actually make different choices.

Follow That French Fry

A publicized study that evaluated and revealed the hidden costs of our current food transport system would enable consumers to weigh the external costs against the benefits and decide for themselves whether they want to pay those costs. A collaborative effort between Departments of Transportation, of Agriculture, of Health, of Economic Development, and of Environmental Quality could show that something as tangible and personal as food, and as abstract and impersonal as roads, are directly connected, at direct cost to the traveling and eating public. Following in Britain's congestion-busting footsteps, states could then create an Annual Food Transport Indicator that would monitor food miles on a yearly basis.[53] A yearly measurement could track changes and monitor progress between transportation infrastructure, vehicle technology, fuel efficiency, agricultural activity, and consumer behavior.

And then what? Assuming a food miles study reveals opportunities for positive change, what sort of solutions should we pursue to implement these changes? A number of possible approaches come to mind, falling into one of two categories: those practices that cover the full costs of long- distance food transport, and those that reduce the number of food-bearing trucks on the roads.

Solutions That Charge for the Roads We Consume

> *"More than ever before, Americans take for granted buying imported fresh fruits, vegetables, and flowers at their local supermarkets; next-day delivery of goods purchased over the Internet; and tracking express packages online to know their whereabouts at any given time."*[54]

So says the United States Department of Transportation in its 2006 analysis of freight movement, "Freight in America: A New National Picture." The same report notes that trucking is the shipping choice for many businesses and is increasing its market share.[55] The anticipated increase in freight traffic, taken together with the shrinking transportation budgets of almost every state, suggests that one major response to measuring the external costs of food transport is to charge the full transportation costs of our food shipments by tolling the food miles used.

Tolling is a user fee approach, as wildly unpopular a funding approach with most consumers as a gas tax increase. Tolling might become more appealing, however, when considered alongside the true costs of food transport. The Truck Only Toll lane (TOT) is one type of tolling scheme currently under consideration in the US by some state and federal governments.[56] TOTs come in a number of forms. They may be regular lanes on existing roadways converted into truck lanes and separated from other traffic by a barrier; lanes elevated above existing roadways; or new construction projects, dedicated to truck traffic alone. The idea in all cases is to separate truck traffic from other traffic and to design roads with the needs of trucks and truckers in mind.

The trucking industry understandably might not want to absorb costs they would incur under a tolled scheme. Shippers exist not for their own sake, but to satisfy the appetites of consumers who purchase the goods trucks bear. So any costs imposed on shippers should be passed on to those who profit most from long-distance trucking: consumers. When goods are priced to include the actual shipping cost, prices will go up, but will only be paid by consumers who buy those goods. Under such a scheme, a coffee aficionado who favors a Kenyan bean would pay the shipping costs for that remotely sourced import, while a McDonald's patron would pay the true costs of a Big Mac whose many ingredients traversed the country perhaps more than once. Neither would pay the transport costs of the other's commodities, as they do today.

On the other hand, some TOTs may be so efficient for trucks that at least some large trucking firms would be willing to pay tolls. A 2002 Reason Foundation policy study, estimated that self-financing Toll Truckways can be designed so specifically for longer combination vehicles (where a single driver carries several times the state-permitted payload) that even after paying tolls, companies can still turn a healthy profit.[57]

Solutions That Reduce Our Appetite for Roads

- *Local Sourcing and Ecolabeling*

Labeling food with a food miles count could incentivize road-friendly consumer behavior. Food ecolabeling programs are gaining popularity in Europe and the US and can identify a food's origin, environmental or social impact, or show miles traveled and transportation mode used. The 2002 Farm Bill included a Country of Origin Labeling requirement,[58] and a Lawrence, Kansas, supermarket, the Community Mercantile (the Merc), has begun its own labeling program called Miles to the Merc that labels the distances food travels to its shelves.[59] Denmark has even been experimenting with a secondary bar code database that shows images of the farm where meat is raised, information on an animal's genetics, feed, medication and slaughter date.[60] Consumers who know how far food has traveled will know how many road miles their choices consume and can more easily choose food that travels shorter distances to reach them.

- *Road-to-Rail Shift*

Though rail played a leading role in the nation's early infrastructure development, by 2000 it moved only 16% of the nation's freight; 78% went by truck.[61] By 1996, 93% of fresh produce transported between cities in the US traveled by truck.[62] Perhaps it is time to relieve our roadways and revitalize our rail lines. Shifting food transport to rail shares the same advantages as shifting any freight to rail: trains emit significantly less pollution,[63] cause far fewer fatalities,[64] cause little highway congestion, and consume far less fuel than trucks.[65] Rail is not as timely as truck transport, so fresh food may spoil more easily traveling by rail. However, increasing local production of fresh food could reduce the need to transport fresh food over long distances.

- *Transport Collaboration and Out of Hours Deliveries*

Transport collaboration is a collaboration between shippers to share the leg of a trip when neither has a full load. A 2007 UK study shows that by combining collaboration between vertical supply chain partners and horizontal collaboration between other logistics service providers, shippers can more easily comply with new, transport-friendly regulation, and can also reduce transport costs.[66] Out of Hours Deliveries, specific to urban environments, help reduce urban congestion during business hours by shifting freight deliveries to non-business hours.

Food has always been a form of cultural exchange, a way to learn about people in other parts of the world. It is hard to argue with the educational benefits of eating a new dish and knowing its cultural origins, different from your own. Part of that education, however, is to discover what can actually be grown in one's own backyard. What cannot be grown locally becomes a treat we pay for, rather than an everyday entitlement we expect.

One Apple at a Time

> *"The solutions to this problem will require commitment by the public, and by national, state and local officials to increase investment levels and identify projects, programs and policies that can achieve mobility goals."*[67]

As congestion experts Tim Lomax and David Schrank point out, the solution to our mobility problems will be a collaborative effort between the public and the government, applied to more than one area of change. Food transport is one of those areas, and government is beginning to play its part. Cities and counties have been declaring official local eating days and weeks and months for the last couple of years. Recently Humboldt County, California, joined the ranks of official local eaters when the County Board of Supervisors announced in 2007 that September was Local Foods Month,[68] and Austin, Texas, proclaimed December 8-15 Eat Local Week.[69] And in British Columbia, Vancouver is taking local eating to a whole new level. The city council will soon consider a proposal to extend a pre-existing set of "urban agriculture" guidelines for high density developments to all new multifamily projects in Vancouver. Those guidelines include edible landscaping and food-producing gardens in shared garden plots, and on rooftops and balconies.[70]

If knowledge is power, why not further arm consumers with information about how their transportation dollars are supporting the food system, and let them decide whether and how they want to spend those dollars? In 2002 trucks bore 90% of the dollar value of US freight[71] and the nation's freight tonnage is expected to increase nearly 70% by 2020.[72] Learning the true cost of food miles could trigger a reduction in the American consumer's appetite for freight in general. For a nation facing a staggering transportation funding gap, measuring food miles might start to look like part of the solution.

Gretchen Stoeltje is a researcher in the Government and Public Affairs Division of the Texas Department of Transporta-

tion (TxDOT). She holds an undergraduate degree in film from the University of California, Santa Cruz, and a law degree from Santa Clara University in Santa Clara, California. She may be reached at gstoelt@dot.state.tx.us or 512.416.2385.

Endnotes

1 Hendrickson, John, "Energy Use in the U.S. Food System: A Summary of Existing Research and Analysis," 2004: 8. University of Wisconsin-Madison, College of Agricultural and Life Sciences, 27 February 2008 http://www.cias.wisc.edu/pdf/energyuse2.pdf.

2 The American Association of State Highway and Transportation Officials (AASHTO), AASHTO Guide for Design of Pavement Structures 1993, (AASHTO 1993), Appendix D.

3 Pirog, Rich and Andrew Benjamin. "Checking the Food Odometer: Comparing Food Miles for Local versus Conventional Produce Sales to Iowa Institutions." July 2003: 4. Leopold Center for Sustainable Agriculture, Iowa State University. 29 February 2008 http://www.leopold.iastate.edu/pubs/staff/files/food_travel072103.pdf.

4 "CBO Testimony: Statement of Donald B. Marron, Deputy Director, Status of the Highway Trust Fund: 2007," March 27, 2007: 1. Congressional Budget Office, 27 February 2008 http://www. cbo.gov/ftpdocs/79xx/doc7909/03-27-Highway_Testimony.pdf.

5 Kelderman, Eric, "The State of the Union – Crumbling," Stateline. Org. 16 January 2008: 2. 11 February 2008 http://www.stateline.org/live/details/story?contentId=270952.

6 Kelderman 1.

7 Sundeen, Matt and James B. Reed, "Surface Transportation Funding: Options for States," 2006: xii. National Conference of State Legislatures, 27 February 2008 http://www.ncsl.org/print/transportation/item014233.pdf.

8 Fisher, Dawn, Andrew Palmer and Alan McKinnon, "Reducing the External Costs of the Domestic Transportation of Food by the Food Industry," 16 April 2007: 0. Faber Maunsell, 27 February 2008 http://statistics.defra.gov.uk/esg/reports/costfoodtransport/Defra Final Report 17 May 2007.pdf.

9 Watkiss, Paul et al, "Validity of Food Miles as an Indicator of Sustainable Development," July 2005: i-ii. AEA Technology, 27 February 2008 http://statistics.defra.gov.uk/esg/reports/foodmiles/final.pdf.

10 Fisher, Palmer and McKinnon 3.

11 Xuereb, Marc, "Food Miles: Environmental Implications of Food Imports to Waterloo Region," November 2005:3. Region of Waterloo Public Health, 27 February 2008 http://chd.region.waterloo.on.ca/web/health.nsf/0/54ED787F44ACA44C852571410056AEB0/$file/FOOD_MILES_REPORT.pdf?openelement.

12 Pirog, Rich, Timothy Van Pelt, Kamyar Enshayan, Ellen Cook, "Food Duel and Freeways: An Iowa Perspective on How Far Food Travels, Fuel Usage and Greenhouse Gas Emissions," June 2001:1. Leopold Center for Sustainable Agriculture, 27 February 2008 <http://www.leopold.iastate.edu/pubs/staff/ppp/food_mil.pdf>.

13 Pirog and Benjamin 4.

14 United States Department of Transportation, Federal Highway Administration, Dwight D. Eisenhower National System of Interstate and Defense Highways. p. 2. 27 February 2008 http://www.fhwa.dot.gov/programadmin/interstate.cfm.

15 TRIP, Keep Both Hands on the Wheel: Metro Areas with the Roughest Rides and Strategies to Make Our Roads Smoother, March 2008: 2. Washington D.C. 12 March 2008. http://www.tripnet.org/RoughRideReportOct2006.pdf.

16 United States Department of Transportation, Federal Highway Administration, Freight Analysis Framework: FAF2 Data and Documentation: 2002-2035. 2007. Interpreted by Tianjia Tang, Office of Freight Management and Operations, Federal Highway Administration in email to author, November 20, 2007.

17 United States Department of Transportation, Federal Highway Administration, Freight Analysis Framework, Tang.

18 AASHTO Appendix D.

19 March , James W., "Federal Highway Cost Allocation Study," Public Roads, Vol. 61, No. 4, January/February 1998: 7. United States Department of Transportation, Federal Highways Administration. 1 February 2008 <http://www.tfhrc.gov/pubrds/janpr/cost.htm>.

20 Schlosser, Eric. Fast Food Nation: The Dark Side of the All-American Meal. 2001:120. Houghton Mifflin Books.

21 Schlosser 111-131.

22 Ungood-Thomas, Jon, "British Prawns go to China to be Shelled," May 20, 2007: 1 The Sunday Times, The TimesOnline. 21 November 2007 http://www.timesonline.co.uk/tol/news/uk/article1813836.ece.

23 Ungood-Thomas 1.

24 Ungood-Thomas 2.

25 Ungood-Thomas 1.

26 Burka, Paul, "The Farm to Market Road," Texas Monthly Magazine. 22 October 2007 http://www.texasmonthly.com/ranch/readme/farm.php.

27 Texas Transportation Institute, "Getting it Built," Texas Transportation Researcher: Mobility and the Environment, Volume 41, Number 4:1. 23 October 2007 http://tti.tamu.edu/publications/researcher/newsletter.htm?vol=41&issue=4&article=9.

28 Ikerd, John "Eating Local: A Matter of Integrity." The Eat Local Challenge Kickoff Event. Eco Trust, Portland, OR. 2 June 2005. Also Sierra Farm Tour and the Alabama Sustainable Agriculture Network Field Day, Banks Alabama. 18 June 2005: 5. 28 February 2008 http://web.missouri.edu/ikerdj/papers/AlabamaEat%20Local.htm.

29 Ikerd 5.

30 Ikerd 5.

31 Illinois Food, Farms and Jobs Act. Pub. Act 095-0145: sec. 5, para. 13. 14 August 2007.

32 Illinois Food, Farms and Jobs Act, Pub. Act 095-0145: sec. 5, para. 2.

33 Texas Department of Agriculture. Texas Agriculture Packs a Punch. Texas Agriculture Facts, Go Texan Program. 12 July 2007 http://www.gotexan.org/gt/channel/render/items/0,1218,1670_ 1693_0_0,00.html.

34 "Farm Marketing" Sustainable Food Center. 8 October 2007: 1 http://www.sustainablefoodcenter.org/AFM_overview.html.

35 Watkiss et al 66-68.

36 Watkiss et al 11.

37 Xuereb 13.

38 Pirog et al "Food, Fuel and Freeways" 18.

39 Energy Information Administration, Emissions of Greenhouse Gases in the United States 2006. November 2007: 11. United States Department of Energy. 28 February 2008 ftp://ftp.eia.doe.gov/pub/oiaf/1605/cdrom/pdf/ggrpt/057306.pdf.

40 Lomax, Tim and David Schrank. The 2007 Urban Mobility Report September 2007:7. Texas Transportation Institute. 28 February 2008 http://tti.tamu.edu/documents/mobility_report_2007_wappx.pdf.

41 Lomax and Schrank 7.

42 Lomax and Schrank 2.

43 Lomax and Schrank 32, 33.

44 Texas Department of Transportation, press release. "TTC-35 Draft Report Refines Study Area and Identifies Project Need. April 2006: 2. 29 February 2008 http://www.dot.state.tx.us/news/0082006.htm.

45 Currier, Christina. Overview of Truck-Only Toll Lane in the United States. Texas Department of Transportation. 7 May 2007:4. 29 February 2008 http://www.dot.state.tx.us/publications/government_and_public_affairs/truck-only_toll_lanes.pdf.

46 Blog contributors. Your Stories. The 100 Mile Diet. 29 February 2008 http://www.100milediet.org/category/your-stories/.

47 Subscription page. Edible Austin. No. 4 Spring 2008:50.

48 OUP Blog. "Oxford Word of the Year: Locavore." 12 November 2007. Oxford University Press. 29 February 2008 http://blog.oup.com/2007/11/locavore.

49 Pirog, Rich, and Andy Larson, "Consumer Perceptions of the Safety, Health, and Environmental Impact of Various Scales and Geographic Origin of Food Supply Chain," September 2007: 4. Leopold Center for Sustainable Agriculture. 29 February 2008 http://www.leopold.iastate.edu/pubs/staff/consumer/consumer_0907.pdf.

50 Pirog and Larson 3.

51 Pollan, Michael. The Omnivore's Dilemma: A Natural History of Four Meals. 11 April 2006: 140-143, 257. The Penguin Press.

52 Schlosser 267-270.

53 Watkiss et al viii.

54 United States Department of Transportation. Freight in America. Research and Innovative Technology Administration, Bureau of Transportation Statistics. January 2006: 1. 29 February 2008 http://www.bts.gov/publications/freight_in_america/pdf/entire.pdf.

55 United States Department of Transportation. Freight in America 1.

56 Currier 3-7.

57 Samuel, Peter, Robert Poole Jr., and José Holguin-Veras, "Toll Truckways: A New Path Toward Safer and More Efficient Freight Transportation," Policy Summary No. 294, Reason Public Policy Institute, 2002:1. Reason Foundation. 29 February 2008 http://www.reason.org/ps294polsum.pdf.

58 Farm Security and Rural Investment Act Of 2002. Pub. L. 107–171. 13 May 2002. 116 Stat. 533.

59 Van Dalsem, Sarah. "Traveling Light: '100-Mile Diet' Limits Pollution, Supports Locally Produced Food," 1 August 2007: 1. Lawrence Journal World and News. 29 February 2008 http://www2.ljworld.com/news/2007/aug/01/traveling_light/.

60 Pollan Omnivore's Dilemma 244.

61 American Association of State Highways and Transportation Officials. Transportation/Invest in America: Freight-Rail Bottom Line. 2007:13. (AASHTO) 29 February 2008 http://freight.transportation.org/doc/FreightRailReport.pdf.

62 Pirog, Van Pelt, Enshayan, Cook 12.

63 AASHTO, Transportation/Invest in America 29.

64 United States Department of Transportation, Federal Highway Administration. Freight Management and Operations, Table 5-1: Transportation Fatalities by Freight Transportation Mode. 11 Febraury 2005. 29 February 2008 http://ops.fhwa.dot.gov/freight/freight_analysis/nat_freight_stats/docs/04factsfigures/table5_1.htm.

65 AASHTO, Transportation/Invest in America 29.

66 Mason, Robert, Chandra Lalwani, Roger Broughton, "Combining Vertical and Horizontal Collaboration for Transport Optimization." Supply Chain Management: An International Journal. 2007:187-188, 196.

67 Lomax and Schrank 1.

68 Doran, Bob "It's Official! Community Alliance Rolls Out Local Foods Month." The North Coast Journal of Politics, People and Art. 6 September 2007. 29 February 2008 http://www.northcoastjournal.com/090607/food0906.html.

69 "Edible Austin Eat Local Week—Dec. 8-15." Edible Austin. 8 November 2007. 29 February 2008 http://www.edibleaustin.com/pages/eatlocal.htm#top.

70 Ramslie, Dave, Sustainability Group Manager, Sustainable Development Program, City of Vancouver. email to the author. 22 February 2007.

71 Samuel, Poole, and Holguin-Veras 1.

72 United States Department of Transportation. Freight in America: A New National Picture. Research and Innovative Technology Administration, Bureau of Transportation Statistics. Washington DC. 2006: 3.

12

Political Forces Make It Difficult for Local Food Economies to Succeed

Michael Pollan and Rod Dreher

Michael Pollan is the Knight Professor of Science and Environmental Journalism at the University of California, Berkeley. He is the author of numerous articles and books, including In Defense of Food: An Eater's Manifesto *and* The Omnivore's Dilemma: A Natural History of Four Meals. *Rod Dreher is an editorial columnist for the* Dallas Morning News *and the author of* Crunchy Cons.

Many experienced farmers would like to move away from large agribusiness models of farming or start up small, sustainable farms, but government regulations and subsidies that favor large farms make it difficult for them to do so. Further, the policies that Americans are told will help farms succeed only help to drive food costs down, which benefits large corporations turning bulk produce into packaged products, and do not benefit small local farms. Americans are also drawn away from the products of smaller farms due to heavy marketing given to packaged products and the higher cost of sustainably produced foods. Clean and safe foods produced through sustainable farming methods and fair labor practices need to be made a priority of our government, political leaders, and of family and community life.

Michael Pollan and Rod Dreher, "Table Talk: Michael Pollan Chats with Rod Dreher About How Food Culture Can Transcend the Left-Right Divide," *The American Conservative*, vol. 7, June 30, 2008, pp. 9–12.

Rod Dreher is the author of *Crunchy Cons*—the book and the Beliefnet blog—and an editorialist for the *Dallas Morning News*. On TAC's [the *American Conservative*'s] behalf, he recently interviewed Michael Pollan, the best-selling author of *The Ominivore's Dilemma: A Natural History of Four Meals* and *In Defense of Food: An Eater's Manifesto*. Pollan's work, like Dreher's, is about more than just eating well—it's also about the health of communities. Dreher's "Birkenstocked Burkeans"—localist libertarians like organic farmer Joel Salatin and young conservatives of many stripes—have increasingly taken an interest in Pollan's writing. So we brought together the original Crunchy Conservative and the defender of real food. Their conversation follows:

Little Support for Changing Food Culture

Rod Dreher: What kind of conservatives do you find are interested in your work about food culture?

Michael Pollan: There is this Joel Salatin, evangelical Christian, libertarian right wing, but there are not a whole lot of them. Frankly, it baffles me that this growing food movement doesn't have more support on the right. It's very consistent with libertarianism, and it is very consistent with family values. Nevertheless, it is often portrayed in the media as a white-wine-sipping, arugula-chopping, liberal politic. Maybe you can answer for me why that is.

It's a point that I've struggled to figure out. I wrote about Salatin, too. He argues, as you do, that the state's collusion with agribusiness has been disastrous. . . .

For the last 40 years at least, our agricultural policy has been driven by an alliance of agribusiness interests and people in Congress. Farm policy has been organized around driving prices down, which is certainly not in the interest of farmers. It's in the interest of people buying their products—Archer

Daniels Midland, Cargill, McDonald's, and Coca-Cola. They are the beneficiaries to the way we've organized our agriculture.

The deck is really stacked against family farmers and people trying to build local food economies.

Some farmers see this; many don't. We have this institution called the Farm Bureau, which is believed to represent farmers, but they do nothing of the kind. They tend to represent agribusiness. And the states, in their regulations, have tended to favor the biggest interests against the people trying to do smaller things like raw-milk operations.

The USDA [U.S. Department of Agriculture] is also very much organized around promoting the interest of the largest meat packers. Four of them control 82 percent of the market, and all the rules are designed for them. Now, I can understand it from their point of view: One inspector at a national beef plant can inspect 400 carcasses in an hour. If you send him to a small regional plant that is only doing four carcasses in a day, that looks like bad business. But in fact, that small plant is supporting farmers in the community and putting out higher quality meat.

So the deck is really stacked against family farmers and people trying to build local food economies. The federal regulatory regime is choking out some really vital start-ups in an important corner of the American economy.

Marketing Dinner

In cultural terms, how has consumer capitalism as applied to food traditions worked to undermine the family and, by extension, the community?

Look at what food marketing does to the family dinner. The American food industry spends $32 billion a year marketing 17,000 new products to us. They are trying very hard to undermine parents' roles as gatekeepers of the family diet. You have kids clamoring for dinners—as described to me by marketers at General Mills—that consist essentially of serial microwaving. Every family member microwaves his own entree and then they kind of cross paths at the table for a little while.

Food marketers work very hard to get us to eat 24/7, and if you look at the images on television, you see families too hurried to cook a meal. They're so busy that all they can do is grab a cereal bar on the way out the door. All of this emphasis on snack food has the effect of eroding the crucial institution of families sitting down together. One of the great blind spots in American conservatism is not appreciating the role of consumer capitalism in eroding values such as the family dinner.

Maintaining Food Traditions

And communal values. You are talking about how food traditions are a social glue. . . .

It's about sitting down and breaking bread among family or friends or even enemies—the rituals of eating together and cooking for people.

Reducing food to fuel or entertainment, which seems to be the goal of so much food marketing, takes away something important. Movements like Slow Food are fighting against this. . . .

It's about sitting down and breaking bread among family or friends or even enemies—the rituals of eating together and cooking for people.

Food Politics

I mention Slow Food in my work and find it ironic that it was started by an Italian Marxist. . . .

Communist.

Yeah. But it's very conservative.

It is. I always saw myself as being to the Left of center, although whenever I write about food or nature, I feel like I am actually to the Right. Somebody just sent me a blog post from the Tory Anarchist—you're mentioned in it, too—that says, "You might call it the Wendell Berry-Michael Pollan Right." I had not seen all those words strung together before, but it points to why this issue mixes up the usual categories—and it should.

I think that this movement will find trends on the right. You see signs of it in Matthew Scully's work coming at animal welfare from the Right, which makes perfect sense as soon as you start reading it.

I think a lot of the problem is with the cultural signifiers, the fact that the movement's DNA comes out of the '60s. I wrote about this in *Omnivore's Dilemma*—the counterculture and its discovery of organic food—but you go back a few decades and organic food is very much a Tory issue in England.

The Real Cost of Food

Well, among conservatives this discussion usually sparks an angry response, curiously enough based on class; this idea that to criticize the way Americans eat or even to propose thinking critically about it is elitist. The most angry letters I've gotten about my work are from fellow conservatives who say, "You're just an elitist. You want to go to Whole Foods, and that's good for you, but don't criticize the way we eat."

I get it from the Left also—"you're promoting the kind of foods that average people can't afford." And the fact is, eating healthy, carefully grown food in this country does cost more. But I think the focus has to be less on that than why the other food is so cheap. The reason is that it's unfairly subsidized—from direct government subsidies in the form of crop subsidies to the kind of support of agribusiness that I was describing earlier to the fact that the companies growing this food are not required to pay the cost of the environmental damage they do. Did you know that if you've got a feedlot and you're polluting local streams, the government will pay you to clean up your mess? That seems deeply unfair to someone trying to do it right.

Obviously, all the public-health expense that goes with lousy food is also not borne by the people producing the food. If you could really internalize all the cost of that 99-cent double cheeseburger at McDonald's, you would be astounded at what an elitist food it is. It's a $10 burger when you add in all the real costs.

When you pay for that supposedly elitist expensive grass-fed hamburger, you are paying the real cost. You are not depending on illegal-immigrant labor. You are not depending on government subsidies.

You could produce a lot of cotton with slave labor, and it was a great deal. But if I'm selling cotton that I paid people a living wage to grow, and it costs ten times more than your cotton, am I the elitist cotton seller? I don't think so.

When you pay for that supposedly elitist expensive grass-fed hamburger, you are paying the real cost. You are not depending on illegal-immigrant labor. You are not depending on government subsidies.

Solving Global Hunger with Local Solutions

The argument you hear is that if we stopped growing food by industrial methods, people would starve. At a time when hunger is an increasingly important global issue, is now really the time to move away from industrial agriculture?

Well, it isn't clear that you couldn't feed people with a more sustainable agriculture. I don't see us moving to a Joel Salatin model all over the country, with all of us fed locally, but the reason is not for lack of land. The reason is lack of farmers.

Industrial agriculture is a Faustian[1] ideal. If you are willing to move to a highly mechanized, monoculture-based agriculture that depends on chemicals, each individual farmer can produce a lot more food. We can't move away from that because we don't have enough farmers to feed ourselves sustainably right now. However, in the rest of the world, there are still plenty of people who want to stay on the land. And supposedly, if the whole world's agriculture could achieve the level of organic agriculture in the West, that would increase productivity 40 percent overall worldwide. So I don't know that the problem is land so much as labor, and in places where you've got the labor, sustainable agriculture deserves a real try. In Joel's model, he gets an immense amount of animal protein off 100 acres of grass. He can out-compete anybody in that system, but it takes three or four guys to do it, whereas a feedlot can produce a lot of meat with very few guys.

We haven't really tried to feed a lot of people organically, and I think that we could do a lot more than we have. But we have driven people off the land over the last 100 years, while we have increased the productivity of each farmer dramatically. I have trouble imagining us going back, although there is a new generation of farmers coming up. We'll see how they do.

Hope for a New Food Economy

The New York Times *reported recently that more and more young people are reading your work and the work of others and going back to the land. The difference between their movement and the '60s counterculture is that it's now financially viable. So isn't there hope for positive change through the free market?*

Yeah. There is a new food economy based on local and artisanal food systems, and the farmers' market movement is providing a real option for small farmers who are close to

1. A magician and alchemist in German legend who sells his soul to the devil in exchange for power and knowledge.

metropolitan areas. Many of these organic farms started as communes. It was a social experiment, more than an economic experiment, and now there is an economics behind it. That's very encouraging.

I think it's a false choice to say we've got to choose one system for growing our food—industrial or organic or grass-fed. It's got to be all of these things. We should create conditions that make it possible to experiment and see what works in the marketplace. If the industrial system is as unsustainable as people have been saying, it is going to fail in some ways, and we still want to be able to eat.

Farmers would much prefer to be growing real food that people are eating and enjoying than industrial raw materials that get turned into high-fructose corn syrup or ethanol.

Farming and Fossil Fuel

Well, the fuel crisis, if it is permanent, could force these sorts of experiments.

That tremendous increase in productivity I described is all about cheap fossil fuel. It's the result of fertilizers made from natural gas, pesticides made from petroleum, and diesel fuel driving all this equipment and processing. To get to a point where one American farmer can feed 126 Americans for a year, it's one farmer plus cheap fossil fuel.

The big move of American agriculture over the last 100 years is from a dependence on photosynthesis and solar energy to a dependence on fossil fuel. If indeed the era of cheap fossil fuel is over, we are going to have to find ways to put our food system back on a solar-energy basis, and those who are ahead in doing that are organic and grass-fed animal farmers. Every calorie you have ever eaten is a product of photosynthesis. So it should be one of the easier parts of our economy to re-solarize, but it will be expensive.

The Farm Bill

We see these big cultural shifts happening on the food front, but still we end up with monstrosities like the recent farm bill. At the legislative level, what practical goals should reformers be working toward?

We definitely need policy changes, and the farm bill we got was a travesty. Farmers would much prefer to be growing real food that people are eating and enjoying than industrial raw materials that get turned into high-fructose corn syrup or ethanol. We need to give them a path out of that commodity system.

We need to make it easier for farmers to convert to sustainable agriculture if they want to.

I'm convinced from my reading that completely deregulating agriculture—removing all subsidies or crop supports—would probably not work. We have been there before—the agricultural depression of the '20s. We need some kind of organized mechanism to help farmers keep from bankrupting themselves by overproducing. . . .

I also think we need to make it easier for farmers to convert to sustainable agriculture if they want to. That means hiring enough meat inspectors so small processing plants can sprout up around the country.

And given the preciousness of arable land, I think we have to take a look at the rules governing the conversion of farmland in the same way that if you want to build on wetlands, you have to meet a very high burden. I know that's not a conservative idea, but if we reach a population of 10 billion, we will really regret all the houses we are putting up on some of the finest land in the world. . . .

How has your work on food culture and tradition changed your politics?

I keep surprising myself. When I follow the logic of natural systems and the history of our food culture, I find myself trying very hard to defend traditional ways of doing things, and I never thought of myself as a traditionalist.

When I look at Slow Food, it has got a Left component—a critique of consumer capitalism—and it's got a Right component—that these traditions contain great communitarian and biologic value and are very important to defend.

Conservatism has changed a lot in the last 50 years. The modern incarnation of it looks a lot different in its full-throated embrace of capitalism and not making distinctions between, say, small enterprise and monopoly enterprise. Both ends of the political spectrum have boxed themselves in to some contradictions.

Last question: Do you see any potential in our fast-evolving political environment for Left-Right coalitions based around food, farming, and environmental issues?

I do, but you have to scrape a little bit and get past these class signifiers—words like "arugula" that in our culture signify a social formation characterized by the sort of East Coast, Ivy League cultural baggage that David Brooks [an American political and cultural commentator] is so good at chronicling.

"Arugula," we should remember, is a marketing term invented by somebody who thought that this very common green, known by farmers all over the Midwest for many years as "rocket," needed to be tuned up and given new appeal. It's a complete marketing creation, and it's completely ruined a very healthy green—at least from a political point of view.

I think there is an enormous amount of political power lying around on the food issue, and I am just waiting for the right politician to realize that this is a great family issue. If that politician is on the right, all the better. I think that would be terrific, and I will support him or her.

13

Government Regulations Favor Big Industrial, Not Small Local, Farms

Megan Phelps and Joel Salatin

Megan Phelps is a writer and editor at Mother Earth News. *Joel Salatin lives in Virginia where he farms and writes regularly for* Acres USA, *the* Stockman Grass Farmer, *and* American Agriculturist. *He is also the author of several books on farming, including* Everything I Want to Do Is Illegal: War Stories from the Local Food Front.

Government officials are the largest obstacle to success for small local farms. Even though locally grown foods are frequently produced on small farms that use sustainable farming methods, raise animals more cleanly and humanely, are more friendly to the environment, and have fair labor practices, government agencies continue to create policies that favor larger farms that do not use these methods. These policies put up unnecessary hurdles and impede the economic success of small farms, thereby disturbing the economic sustainability and beauty of small farming communities. Despite these challenges, farmers can succeed if they are creative. The public is becoming more interested in knowing the source of the foods they consume, and there is a growing market of people who want to avoid issues such as contaminated food and unethical treatment of animals, which can plague even certified organic farms.

Joel Salatin is a farmer at the forefront of the trend toward local food and grass-fed meat. Many people first became familiar with Salatin's complex and eco-minded approach to farming when he was featured in Michael Pollan's best-selling book, *The Omnivore's Dilemma: A History of Four Meals.* But Salatin also is well known within pasture-based farming and libertarian circles. He's especially vocal about government regulations that make life difficult for the small farmer—his most recent book is titled *Everything I Want to Do Is Illegal: War Stories from the Local Food Front.* He's also the author of *You Can Farm* and *Holy Cows and Hog Heaven.* Salatin kindly agreed to answer some questions for us about Polyface Farm [a farm in Virginia that is run by Salatin and his family]. Hold onto your hat! Here are Salatin's candid thoughts on government regulations, high grain prices, vegetarians and making money at farming.

Grass-Fed and Beyond Organic

Tell us a little bit about Polyface Farm.

We're located eight miles southwest of Staunton, Va., in the Shenandoah Valley on 550 acres (100 open and 450 forest). We also lease four farms, totaling an additional 900 acres of pasture. We sell "salad bar" (grass-fed) beef; "pigaerator" pork; pastured poultry, both broilers and turkeys; pastured eggs and forage-based rabbits.

Your livestock and poultry are grass-fed, and your farm is "beyond organic." Do you find people are familiar with those terms?

More and more people are aware of the compromise and adulteration within the government-sanctioned organic certified community. Weary of 6,000-hen confinement laying houses with three feet of dirt strip being labeled "certified organic," patrons latch onto the "beyond organic" idea. It resonates with their disappointment over the government program. When Horizon battles [Organic] Cornucopia [Family

Farm], for instance, to keep its organic-certified industrial-scale dairies, consumer confidence falls.

Intuitively, people understand that the historical use of the word "organic" identified an idea and a paradigm rather than a visceral list of dos and don'ts. And now that the high prices have attracted unscrupulous growers who enter the movement for the money, people realize that no system can regulate integrity. That is why we have a 24 hour a day, 7 day a week, 365 day a year open-door policy. Anyone is welcome to visit at anytime to see anything, anywhere. Integrity can only be assured with this level of transparency.

When someone asks if we're certified organic, we respond playfully: "Why would we want to stop there? We go beyond organic." That response generally leads to an info-dense discussion and people come away with renewed awareness, rather than just another case of hardening of the categories.

How has the public's attitude toward your products changed in the last few years? Do you find it easier to sell grass-fed meat now?

Public awareness is definitely up. In the 1970s when I was selling grass-finished beef and pastured poultry, nobody had even heard of the word "organic," much less "grass finished." Now, thanks to *New York Times* best-selling authors like Jo Robinson and Michael Pollan, the awareness is huge.

Every time industrial food hiccups with recalls and more diseases, another wave of opt-outers hits the local, integrity food scene. Exciting times.

The market limitations are primarily twofold. One is the supply. The artistry and choreography required to move animals around on palatable pasture year-round in any given bioregion takes years to learn. This is not cookie-cutter rations formulated from annuals stored in a big grain bin. The producer deals with on-farm variables such as seasonality, wet, dry, hot, cold, genetic physiology, minerals, and a host of others. Beyond that, the [USDA] Food Safety and Inspection Service has successfully annihilated most community-based, appropriately sized abattoirs (slaughterhouses) and criminalized on-farm processing. This is by far the major impediment to the local integrity of food.

That's all on the production/processing end. The second market limitation has to do with entry-level requirements for major marketing channels. From liability insurance to net-90-day payment to slotting fees, large buyers share a Wall Street business mentality. That mentality aggressively shuns competition, especially from little innovators. But every time industrial food hiccups with recalls and more diseases, another wave of opt-outers hits the local, integrity food scene. Exciting times.

Deciding to Farm

When did you decide you wanted to be a farmer?

As early as I can remember, I've wanted to be a farmer. I love growing things. I appreciate the emotional steadiness of animals. Every day when I go to move the cow herd, they are glad to see me. The pigs always come over to talk. None of these critters ever asks you to fill out licenses or threatens litigation. They never talk behind your back or conspire to overthrow you. And to watch the land heal, with ever-growing mounds of earthworm castings, is better than any video. Indeed, walking through a dew-speckled pasture in the early morning after a blessed nighttime thunderstorm, the ground literally covered with copulating earthworms—what could be more magical than that?

I had my own laying hen flock at ten years old, pedaling eggs on my bicycle to neighbors, selling them to families in church. The fast-paced, frenzied urban life disconnected from the ponds, the trees and the pasture never held much allure for me. Go away? Why? Where? I think I was planted here. I think God tends my soul here. It's not for everyone, but it satiates my soul with wonder and gratitude.

What's changed about your philosophy of farming over the years?

Like all geezers, I've learned a lot just through experience. Because I'm a third generation Christian-libertarian-environmentalist-capitalist lunatic I don't have a conversion epiphany to share. I've just always been weird.

Initially, I thought I would need to work off-farm to stay here, and I learned that wasn't true. I encourage young people to follow their passion and go ahead and jump. If you wait until all the stars line up, you'll never do it. In recent years, I'd say my biggest change has been regarding economies of scale and marketing realities. Twenty years ago my vision for the food system in Virginia was thousands of little mom and pop farms like ours serving their neighbors. I no longer think that is viable for two reasons. First, urban centers would be hard-pressed to grow all their own food within their communities. Second, most farmers are marketing Neanderthals. Either they really don't want to be around people, or they don't know how to interact with them. A successful marketer needs to be a bit theatrical; a storyteller, schmoozer, gregarious type. And that's not typical, especially among John Deere jockeys.

What's the answer? I don't know, but what I've come up with is what I call food clusters. These require production, processing, marketing, accounting, distribution and customers—these six components make a whole. The cluster can be farmer-driven, customer-driven, even distribution-driven initially. But once these six components are in place, it can micro-duplicate the industrial on a bioregional or food-shed scale, which includes urban centers. I think a local integrity food system could supplant the opaque industrial one in Virginia, but realistically it would comprise several hundred or a thousand \$5–\$10 million food clusters rather than several thousand mom and pop \$100,000 fully integrated enterprises. I certainly never thought our farm would top $1 million in annual sales, but it happened. We still have no business plan or marketing targets. But we've been blessed with a family of enough variety to put together these six foundations for a whole, and that has made all the difference. And I'm a schmoozer.

The on-farm hurdles we've faced, from drought to predators to flood and cash flow, are nothing compared to the emotional, economic and energy drain caused by government bureaucrats.

Government Hurdles

What are some of the biggest challenges you've faced as a farmer?

Anyone familiar with me would have to smile at this question, knowing that my answer would be and continues to be the food police. The on-farm hurdles we've faced, from drought to predators to flood to cash flow, are nothing compared to the emotional, economic and energy drain caused by government bureaucrats. Even in the early 1970s when, as a young teen, I operated a farm stand at the curb market, precursor of today's farmers' markets, the government said I couldn't sell milk. The first business plan I came up with to become a full-time farmer centered around milking ten cows and selling the milk to neighbors at regular retail supermarket prices. It would have been a nice living. But it's illegal. In fact, in 2007 I finally wrote *Everything I Want to Do Is Illegal*, documenting my run-ins with government officials.

I think it's amazing that in a country that promotes the freedom to own firearms, freedom to worship and freedom of speech, we don't have the freedom to choose our own food. If I can't choose the proper fuel to feed my body, I won't have energy to go shoot, preach and pray anyway. Half the alleged food in the supermarket is really dangerous to your health. In fact, if we removed all the food items in the supermarket that would not have been available before 1900, the shelves would be bare. Gone would be all the unpronounceable gobbledy-syllabic industrial additives, irradiated, GMO [genetically modified organism], cloned pseudo-food.

The reason this issue is hard to articulate is because most people don't realize what's not on the shelves, or in their diet. We're fast losing the memory of heritage food, as in made from scratch, in the home kitchen, with culture-wide generic culinary wisdom. I remember when every mom knew how to cut up a chicken. Now, most people don't know a chicken has bones. As the food police have demonized and criminalized neighbor-to-neighbor food commerce, the food system has become enslaved by the industrial food fraternity. And just around the corner is the National Animal Identification System (NAIS) coming on strong, under the guise of food safety and biosecurity, which will annihilate thousands of nonindustrial farms. We don't need programs; we need freedom. If we really had freedom, farmers like me would run circles around the corporate-welfare, food-adulterated, land-abusing industrial farms.

If we really had freedom, farmers like me would run circles around the corporate-welfare, food-adulterated, land-abusing industrial farms.

Raising Healthy Animals, Healthy Meat

What are some of the things you want people to know about the meat they buy from you? What should we all know about the meat we eat?

The main idea we promote is that our animals enjoy a habitat that allows them to fully express their physiological distinctiveness. I like to say we want our pigs to express their pigness and the chickens their chickenness. The industrial food system views plants and animals as inanimate protoplasmic structure to be manipulated, however cleverly the human mind can conceive to manipulate it.

I would suggest that a society that views its life from that egocentric, disrespectful, manipulative standpoint will view its citizenry the same way . . . and other cultures. How we respect and honor the least of these creates the ethical, moral framework on which we honor and respect the greatest of these. The freedom for you to express your Tomness or Maryness is directly proportional to the value society places on the pig expressing its pigness. And to think that our tax dollars are being spent right now to isolate the porcine stress gene in order to extract it from pig DNA so that we can further abuse and dishonor pigs, but at least they won't care. Is that the kind of moral framework on which a civilized society rests? I suggest not.

This fundamental understanding drives our production models. Herbivores in nature do not eat dead cows, chicken manure, dead chickens, grain or silage: They eat fresh or dried forage. Of course, what's neat is that empirical data is discovering the nutritional and ecological benefits of this paradigm. We're reading about Omega-3 and Omega-6 balance, conjugated linoleic acid, polyunsaturated fats and riboflavin. Whenever a new laboratory confirmation of our philosophy hits the news, we make sure our patrons know about it. In a word, this is all about healing: healing our bodies, healing our economies, healing our communities, healing our families, healing the landscape, healing the earthworms. If it's not healing, it's not appropriate.

Perhaps because it's such a hot topic, let me address the cow–global warming argument. Every bit of the alleged science linking methane and cows to global warming is predicated on annual cropping, feedlots and herbivore abuse. It all crumbles if the production model becomes like our mob-stocking-herbivorous-solar-conversion-lignified-carbon-sequestration fertilization. America has traded 73 million bison requiring no petroleum, machinery or fertilizer for 45 million beef cattle, and we think we're efficient. Here at Polyface, we practice biomimicry and have returned to those lush, high- organic-matter production models of the native herbivores.

If every cow producer in the country would use this model, in less than ten years we would sequester all the carbon that's been emitted since the beginning of the industrial age. It's really that simple. Without question, grass-finished, mob-stocked beef is the most efficacious way to heal the planet. We should drastically drop our chicken and pork consumption and return to our indigenous, climate-appropriate protein source: perennial forages turned into red meat and milk.

Vegetarians

Do vegetarians ever challenge you about raising meat? If so, what do you say in response?

I will answer this in two parts. The first has to do with the people who think a fly is a chicken is a child is a cat—what I call the cult of animal worship. This would include the people who think we've evolved beyond the barbaric practice of killing animals to some cosmic nirvana state where killing is a thing of the past.

Rather than indicating a new state of evolutionary connectedness, it actually shows a devolutionary state of disconnectedness. A Bambi-ized culture in which the only human-animal connection is a pet soon devolves into jaundiced foolishness. This philosophical and nutritional foray into a supposed brave new world is really a duplicitous experiment into the anti-indigenous. This is why we enjoy having our patrons come out and see the animals slaughtered. Actually, the seven- to 12-year-old children have no problem slitting throats while their parents cower inside their Prius listening to "All Things Considered." Who is really facing life here? The chickens don't talk or sign petitions. We honor them in life, which is the only way we earn the right to ask them to feed us—like the mutual respect that occurs between the cape buffalo and the lion. To these people, I don't argue. This is a religion and I pretty much leave it alone.

The second part of this answer deals with folks who don't eat meat in order to vote against animal abuse, concentrated animal feeding operations, or pathogenicity. And to be sure, many of these folks have bought into the environmental degradation inherent in livestock farming. To these people, Polyface is a ray of hope. I could write a book about the patrons who have come to us at death's doorstep because they needed meat, and we've watched them heal. To be sure, not everyone needs meat, and those who do have varying levels of need. And when people find out that grass-based livestock offer the most efficacious approach to planetary health, their guilt gives way to compensatory indulgence. After all, they have to make up for lost time, and routinely become our best customers. Their emaciated vegetarian faces fill out, their strength improves and they are happier. Sometimes the easiest thing to do is to just give them a Weston A. Price Foundation brochure. We keep them in our sales building like religious tracts. Oops.

Surviving the Grain Price Increases

How have you been affected (or not affected) by the recent increase in grain prices?

This depends on which species we're talking about. Let's start with the poultry. Broilers will pick up only 15 percent of their diet off the pasture; layers 20 percent; turkeys 30 percent or more. Since birds are omnivores, they can't survive on grass alone. Waterfowl jump on up to more than 50 percent. We've watched our local genetically modified-free grains double in price over the last 24 months. In response, we've raised our chicken and egg prices about 25 percent. Grain is only a portion of the cost, so all we have to do is raise the price enough to compensate for the grain. The amount required to cover these exceptionally high grain prices only amounts to less than $2 per bird. A family buying 50 chickens a year would only pay an additional $100 to cover all the additional feed costs. Of course, the industrial food poultry giants say they can't pass along these costs to their customers. I don't know why, but I think it has to do with the idea that people will only pay so much for junk.

Typically, hogs are similar to chickens, but here at Polyface we're making an end run by finishing pigs on acorns. Just in the nick of time, we discovered an efficient, cheap way to fence out sections of forest with electric fence. Using quarter-inch nylon rope as poor-boy insulators, we zigzag a single 12.5 gauge Tipper Tie aluminum wire from tree to tree and erect three- to five-acre finishing glens. In our native Appalachian oak forests, each acre displaces $500 worth of grain. That translates to about $50 per hog in expense, which is enormous. It has allowed us to keep our hog prices fairly stable even with the huge increase in grain prices. We put the pigs in for one month and remove them for 11 to rest and to let the next acorn crop fall. It actually helps the trees, because the pigs root out competing brush and brambles for their starchy roots, in effect weeding the woodlot. All parties win. Very exciting. And if you think about the millions of acres of forests and realize that they could displace tilled, petroleum-based, subsidized, annual grain cropland, you begin to see the potential of this model.

Finally, salad bar beef. This is the most exciting, because it is completely immune to grain prices. It requires no tillage, no fertilizer, no feed transportation or drying costs. It runs on real-time solar energy, self-harvesting with four-wheel drive self-propelled sauerkraut tanks. At Polyface, we believe we've become the least-cost producer in an artisanal market, which pushes the gross margin both ways. That's pretty cool. As a result, we have not raised our beef prices at all, and are watching with great satisfaction the squirming and postulating within the feedlot industry. They don't need any bailouts. Let them die. To place all of this in historical context, we should all realize that until cheap energy, beef was always the cheapest meat while pork and poultry were the luxuries—especially poultry. When President [Franklin Delano] Roosevelt said his vision for America included "a chicken in every pot," he was talking about today's filet mignon. With cheap fuel, cheap grain, cheap labor and cheap pharmaceuticals came cheap poultry. In the continuum of human history, poultry cheaper than beef is a veritable blip. For nutritional, environmental and social reasons, I think it would be fine for the historical beef-poultry relationship to be restored. And most things do eventually find a way of coming home.

Local Sales

Describe some of the ways you sell your products. You've made it a general principle not to ship anything, but there are several ways you sell products locally.

We have three marketing venues: farm gate, restaurant/retail and metropolitan buying clubs. For the farm gate sales, we send out a newsletter once a year, in the spring, and patrons order for the season from that schedule. We used to sell everything that way, but with frenzied schedules and gas prices, resistance to driving out to the farm started becoming an issue. We live way out in the boonies on a dirt road where the only time you have to lock your car is in August to keep the neighbors from putting runaway zucchini squash in it. This still accounts for 30 percent of our sales. We have public hours, 9 to 4 every Saturday, and that allows us to serve the non-ordering people without sales interruptions throughout the week. Our simple sales building contains scales, freezers and counters to handle these customers.

Restaurant/retail we lump together because we deliver to them on Thursdays and Fridays every week, and they pay about the same prices—a bit of a volume discount. A delivery fee per pound and scaled to volume pays for a vehicle and driver. Several nearby cheese, produce, mushroom and honey growers add their wares to our delivery bus and that helps the distribution economies of scale. We service about 25 upscale restaurants and about ten retail venues, primarily specialty foodie-type businesses. My daughter-in-law, Sheri, calls these patrons on Tuesday for that week's orders. Several restaurants in Washington, D.C., use an independent courier to come to the farm and deliver their orders. Among these restaurants is one fast-food establishment: the Charlottesville branch of the national Chipotle chain. This has been a huge undertaking for both of us, but heralds a new awareness of local and ecologically sound food. These venues account for 30 percent of our sales.

The metropolitan buying clubs grew serendipitously out of quarterly farm gate sales from three Maryland patrons who asked us to deliver to their area for all their friends who would not make the trek to the farm. This has grown to 20 drop points and we deliver to them eight times per year. The same delivery driver and infrastructure that services the restaurants services these patrons. They order via electronic shopping cart. Each drop point must average an annual sales quota and patrons are rewarded with free product for bringing in new customers. This venue provides neighborhood service, low overhead and complete inventory shopping options. We don't deal with farmers' market commissions, rules, product speculation or politics. It's the ultimate marketing below the radar and keeps us out of the supermarket, with its slotting fees, red tape and tardy invoice payments. This venue now accounts for 40 percent of our annual sales.

We hope to add an additional venue in the next few months. Sysco via abattoir. In the summer of 2008, we (my wife Teresa and I) along with a partner purchased our local federal-inspected abattoir, T&E Meats, in Harrisonburg, Va.

Institutional demand for local, humane and ecological products is growing, but vending contracts preclude purchasing outside large distributor channels. For example, University of Virginia contracts its dining services to Aramark, which contracts its food vending to Sysco. But Sysco requires $3 million liability insurance, hold harmless agreements and other forms before purchasing from anyone. This is a serious impediment to local producers. Having acquired this abattoir, however, we hope to use its high product liability policy as a backdoor entry into the institutional market. Stay tuned.

Difficulties for New Farmers

You've done a lot of work encouraging other people to learn to farm through your books and your apprenticeship program. What are some of the challenges you think that new farmers will have to face?

The first and greatest challenge is experience—how to do more with less and how to solve problems creatively rather than with something purchased. Land is more available now than it has been in decades. With half of America's farmland due to change hands in the next 15 years due to the aging farmer, a lot of this land will be available for management at extremely modest cost, owned by family members who aren't ready to sell, or by new e-boom buyers able to afford to buy. In any case, the weak link will be a track record and experience to take a piece of raw land and make it profitable.

I think the opportunities are practically unprecedented. We had an apprentice leave two years ago and within three months had offers for 1,000 acres to manage in New York—at virtually no cost except to use it and keep it aesthetically and aromatically romantic. That's what healing farming is all about, and why it has so much possibility. What landlord wants a Tyson chicken house built on their farm? But all of them love a pastoral setting, especially being able to entertain their city business partners with grass-finished steaks on the porch overlooking your herd of cows. The problem is that our culture tells bright, bushy-tailed young people that farming is for backward, D-student, tobacco-chewing, trip-over-the-transmission-in-the-front-yard, redneck Bubbas.

When was the last time you heard a group of parents bragging? Ever hear one say, "Well, you can have your doctors, lawyers, accountants and engineers. My kid is going to grow up and be a farmer." Ever hear that? Not on your life. The biggest obstacle is emotional—overcoming the cultural prejudice against splinters and blisters. That is why I talk about economics and marketing, along with the mystical, artistic elements of the farm. Yes, it's a lot of work. But what a great office. What a noble life. What a sacred calling.

Organizations to Contact

The editors have compiled the following list of organizations concerned with the issues debated in this book. The descriptions are derived from materials provided by the organizations. All have publications or information available for interested readers. The list was compiled on the date of publication of the present volume; names, addresses, phone and fax numbers, and e-mail and Internet addresses may change. Be aware that many organizations take several weeks or longer to respond to inquiries, so allow as much time as possible.

Community Alliance with Family Farmers (CAFF)
PO Box 363, Davis, California 95617
(530) 756-8518 • fax: (530) 756-7857
e-mail: info@caff.org
Web site: www.caff.org

The Community Alliance with Family Farmers (CAFF) is a collaborative effort of farmers and urban activists to build a movement of rural and urban people to foster family-scale agriculture that cares for the land, sustains local economies, and promotes social justice. CAFF publishes the quarterly *Agrarian Advocate*, which is available on its Web site.

Community Food Security Coalition (CFSC)
3830 SE Division Street, Portland, OR 97202
(503) 954-2970 • fax: (503) 954-2959
Web site: www.foodsecurity.org

The Community Food Security Coalition (CFSC) is dedicated to building strong, sustainable, local, and regional food systems that ensure access to affordable, nutritious, and culturally appropriate food for all people. CFSC seeks to develop self-reliance among all communities in obtaining their food and to create a system of growing, manufacturing, processing, making available, and selling food that is regionally based and grounded in the principles of justice, democracy, and sustainability. CFSC hosts an annual conference and publishes a newsletter, reports, informational handouts, and books on food issues, all of which can be found on its Web site.

Edible Communities

369 Montezuma Avenue, Suite 577, Santa Fe, NM 87501
(505) 989-8822 • fax: (505) 989-7900
Web site: www.ediblecommunities.com

Edible Communities is a publishing and information services company that creates community-based, local food publications in distinct culinary regions throughout the United States, Canada, and Europe. Through its publications, supporting Web sites, and events, Edible Communities connects consumers with family farmers, growers, chefs, and food artisans of all kinds. The Web site contains links to articles, other local food publications, and to the regional Edible Communities publications.

Family Farm Defenders (FFD)

1019 Williamson Street #B, Madison, WI 53703
(608) 260-0900
e-mail: familyfarmdefenders@yahoo.com
Web site: www.familyfarmdefenders.org

Family Farm Defenders exists to create a farmer-controlled and consumer-oriented food system that empowers farmers to advocate for social and economic justice. FFD has worked to create opportunities for farmers to join together in new cooperative endeavors, form a mutual marketing agency, and forge alliances with consumers through providing high-quality food products while returning a fair price to the farmers. The Web site contains links to statements, letters, and other sources of information on topics such as the national animal identification system, farm workers rights, fair trade, and local food systems.

FoodRoutes Network (FRN)
RR #1 Box 25, Troy, PA 16947
(570) 673-3398
e-mail: info@foodroutes.org
Web site: www.foodroutes.org

The FoodRoutes Network (FRN) works to provide communications tools, technical support, and networking and information resources to organizations nationwide that work to rebuild local, community-based food systems. FRN developed the "Buy Fresh Buy Local" program to support sustainable food and farming systems. It publishes information about the benefits of buying local and maintains on its Web site a library of recent reports, publications, video clips, and audio files on topics including health, food safety, and the environment.

Food Trust
One Penn Center, Suite 900, 1617 John F. Kennedy Boulevard
Philadelphia, PA 19103
(215) 575-0444 • fax: (215) 575-0466
e-mail: contact@thefoodtrust.org
Web site: www.thefoodtrust.org

The Food Trust works with neighborhoods, schools, grocers, farmers and policy makers to make healthy food more easily available to all. The Food Trust is home to several school- and community-based projects and offers consulting services to organizations and individuals. The Web site contains detailed information on its projects as well as links to reports, articles, and recent news.

Institute for Agriculture and Trade Policy (IATP)
2105 First Avenue South, Minneapolis, MN 55404
(612) 870-0453 • fax: (612) 870-4846
Web site: www.iatp.org

The Institute for Agriculture and Trade Policy (IATP) works to build thriving local food systems by strengthening small- and medium-scale sustainable farms, expanding market opportunities for farmers, creating innovative partnerships, and advancing supportive policy change. Some of its programs include bringing local and sustainably grown foods into schools, hosting farmers' markets, and bringing locally grown food into urban areas. The Web site contains numerous reports, articles, press releases, and fact sheets.

Land Institute
2440 East Water Well Road, Salina, KS 67401
(785) 823-5376 • fax: (785) 823-8728
e-mail: info@landinstitute.org
Web site: www.landinstitute.org

The Land Institute is a nonprofit research and education organization working to develop the Natural Systems Agriculture to improve ecological stability, promote community relationships, and increase crop yield. It collaborates with public institutions to direct more research to agricultural systems. The institute has published numerous articles, many of which are available on its Web site. The Web site also contains relevant links, bibliographies, and is the home to the Prairie Writers Circle, which brings together writers who produce op-ed commentary to encourage wider public awareness of ecological and sustainability issues important to the organization's mission.

La Via Campesina
Jl. Mampang Prapatan XIV No. 5, Jakarta Selatan
DKI Jakarta 12790
Indonesia
+62-21-7991890 • fax: +62-21-7993426
Web site: www.viacampesina.org

The principal objective of La Via Campesina is to develop solidarity and unity among small farmer organizations in order to promote social justice with fair economic relations; the preservation of land, water, seeds, and other natural resources; food sovereignty; and sustainable agricultural production based on small- and medium-sized producers. The Web site contains information on La Via Campesina's conferences; links to its reports, informational leaflets, and other published information; and provides global news updates and additional information on food, farming, the environment, and human rights.

Local Harvest (LH)

220 Twenty-first Avenue, Santa Cruz, CA 95062
(831) 475-8150 • fax: (831) 401-2418
e-mail: erin@localharvest.org
Web site: www.localharvest.org

Local Harvest (LH) exists to help people find products from family farms and local sources of sustainably grown food and to connect small farms with local consumers. LH maintains a public nationwide directory of small farms, farmers' markets, and other local food sources. The Web site also contains a forum, member blogs, and a newsletter.

National Family Farm Coalition (NFFC)

110 Maryland Avenue NE, Suite 307, Washington, DC 20002
(202) 543-5675 • fax: (202) 543-0978
e-mail: nffc@nffc.net
Web site: www.nffc.net

The National Family Farm Coalition (NFFC) serves as a national link for grassroots organizations working on family farm issues. The goal of NFFC is to assist member groups to secure sustainable, economically just, healthy, safe, and secure food and farm systems. The Web site contains information about many aspects of farming, including factory farming, trade, and the farm bill.

Organic Consumers Association (OCA)

6771 South Silver Hill Drive, Finland, MN 55603
(218) 226-4164 • fax: (218) 353-7652
Web site: www.organicconsumers.org

The Organic Consumers Association (OCA) is a grassroots organization campaigning for health, justice, and sustainability. The OCA deals with crucial issues of food safety, industrial agriculture, genetic engineering, children's health, corporate accountability, fair trade, environmental sustainability, and other key topics. OCA produces a weekly e-mail publication, *Organic Bytes*, as well as a semi-annual newsletter, *Organic View*, both of which are available on the Web site. The site also contains additional information on a variety of topics, including local farms and farm politics.

Slow Food USA

20 Jay Street, Suite M04, Brooklyn, NY 11201
(718) 260-8000 • fax: (718) 260-8068
e-mail: info@slowfoodusa.org
Web site: www.slowfoodusa.org

Slow Food USA is a nonprofit educational organization dedicated to supporting and celebrating the food traditions of North America through programs and activities dedicated to taste education, defending biodiversity, and building food communities. Slow Food USA seeks to reconnect Americans with the people, traditions, plants, animals, fertile soils, and waters that produce foods and create change in the food system. The Web site contains links to local Slow Food chapters, where users can view newsletters, find events, and view articles related to their regions.

Sustainable Table

215 Lexington Avenue, Suite 1001, New York, NY 10016
(212) 991-1930 • fax: (212) 726-9160
e-mail: info@sustainabletable.org
Web site: www.sustainabletable.org

Sustainable Table was created to help consumers understand the problems with our food supply and offer viable solutions and alternatives that celebrate the joy of food and eating. The Web site contains the Eat Well Guide, a free, online directory of sustainably raised meat, poultry, dairy, and eggs from farms, stores, restaurants, bed and breakfasts, and other outlets across the United States and Canada.

WHY
505 Eighth Avenue, Suite 2100, New York, NY 10018
(800) 548-6479
Web site: www.whyhunger.org

WHY works to eradicate hunger and poverty in the United States and around the world through grassroots movements, including those that assist small farmers and teach people to grow their own food. The Web site contains information on numerous topics related to farming, including local food, nutrition, and rural poverty. There are also links to commentary on recent local food news.

Bibliography

Books

Geoff Andrews	*The Slow Food Story: Politics and Pleasure*. Montreal, Quebec: McGill-Queen's University Press, 2008.
Lou Bendrick	*Eat Where You Live: How to Find and Enjoy Fantastic Local and Sustainable Food No Matter Where You Live*. Seattle, WA: Skipstone, 2008.
Samuel Fromartz	*Organic, Inc.: Natural Foods and How They Grew*. Orlando, FL: Harcourt Books, 2006.
Brian Halweil	*Eat Here: Homegrown Pleasures in a Global Supermarket*. New York: W.W. Norton, 2004.
Daniel Imhoff	*Food Fight: The Citizen's Guide to a Food and Farm Bill*. Healdsburg, CA: Watershed Media, 2007.
Barbara Kingsolver, Steven L. Hopp, and Camille Kingsolver	*Animal, Vegetable, Miracle: A Year of Food Life*. New York: HarperCollins, 2007.
Gaston T. LaBue, ed.	*Hunger in America: Issues and Assistance*. New York: Nova Science Publishing, Inc., 2009.

James E. McWilliams *Just Food: Where Locavores Get It Wrong and How We Can Truly Eat Responsibly*. New York: Little, Brown and Co., 2009.

Gary Paul Nabhan *Coming Home to Eat: The Pleasures and Politics of Local Food*. New York: W.W. Norton, 2009.

Michael Pollan *In Defense of Food: An Eater's Manifesto*. New York: Penguin, 2008.

Michael Pollan *The Omnivore's Dilemma: A Natural History of Four Meals*. New York: Penguin, 2006.

Jill Richardson *Recipe for America: Why Our Food System Is Broken and What We Can Do to Fix It*. Brooklyn, NY: Ig Publishing, 2009.

Joel Salatin *Everything I Want to Do Is Illegal: War Stories from the Local Food Front*. Swoope, VA: Polyface, 2007.

Peter Singer and Jim Mason *The Ethics of What We Eat: Why Our Food Choices Matter*. New York: Rodale, 2006.

Alisa Smith and J.B. MacKinnon *Plenty: Eating Locally on the 100-Mile Diet*. New York: Three Rivers Press, 2007.

Periodicals

Brita Belli "Local Is the New Organic," *E: The Environmental Magazine*, March 2007.

Javier Blas and Jenny Wiggins	"Food Companies Put Sustainability on the Menu," *Financial Times*, November 12, 2009.
Grace Lee Boggs	"Food for All: How to Grow Democracy: Detroit's 'Quiet Revolution,'" *Nation*, September 21, 2009.
Marian Burros	"How to Eat (and Read) Close to Home," *New York Times*, August 29, 2007.
John Cloud	"Eating Better Than Organic," *Time*, March 2, 2007.
Gilbert M. Gaul and Dan Morgan	"A Slow Demise in the Delta: U.S. Farm Subsidies Favor Big over Small, White over Black," *Washington Post*, June 20, 2007.
Pallavi Gogoi	"Innovation on the Farm," *BusinessWeek*, May 21, 2008. www.buinessweek.com.
Jerry Hagstrom	"Farm Bill Provided Roots for Local Food Promotion Effort," *Congress Daily AM*, October 20, 2009.
Rich Heffern	"Healthy Eating vs. Feeding the World: Our Food System Figures into Health Care Reform Debate," *National Catholic Reporter*, October 30, 2009.
Michael Hill	"As Local Food Gains, Local Planners Face Decisions," Associated Press, November 4, 2009.

Wes Jackson and Wendell Berry	"A 50-Year Farm Bill," *New York Times*, January 4, 2009.
Paul D. Johnson	"Voting with Your Fork: There Are Good Reasons for Buying Organic and Local," *National Catholic Reporter*, August 21, 2009.
Renée Johnson	"What Is the Farm Bill?" *CRS Report for Congress*, September 23, 2008.
Hugh Joseph	"A Pro-Food Farm Bill," *Boston Globe*, July 9, 2007.
Corby Kummer	"Graze Locally: Shoppers Are Finding More Ways to Buy Humanely Raised Meat from Close-to-Home Farms," *Atlantic*, May 1, 2009.
Terra Lawson-Remer	"The U.S. Farm Bill and the Global Food Crisis," *Huffington Post*, May 29, 2008.
James E. McWilliams	"The Locavore Myth: Why Buying from Nearby Farmers Won't Save the Planet," *Forbes*, August 3, 2009.
Ann Monroe	"The Cost of Eating Green," *MSN Money*, December 17, 2007.
Lindsey Nair	"Local Food Movement Still Gaining Momentum," *Roanoke Times* (Roanoke, VA), September 13, 2009.
Plenty	"Some Interesting Locavore Statistics," March 24, 2009. www.plentymag.com.

Michael Pollan "You Are What You Grow," *New York Times Magazine*, April 22, 2007.

Terry Pristin "With a Little Help, Greens Come to Low-Income Neighborhoods," *New York Times*, June 16, 2009.

Paul Roberts "Farming for Real," *Wilson Quarterly*, Summer 2009.

Margot Roosevelt "Local-Food Movement: The Lure of the 100-Mile Diet," *Time*, June 12, 2006.

Elizabeth Royte "And on Your Left, a Grass-Fed Cow," *OnEarth*, Fall 2007.

Sally Schuff "USDA Lists Farm Bill Priorities," *Feedstuffs*, April 20, 2009.

Kim Severson "When 'Local' Makes It Big," *New York Times*, May 12, 2009.

Joseph B. Treaster "United Nations Food Leader on Defeating Hunger," *Huffington Post*, November 28, 2009.

Bryan Walsh "Getting Real About the High Price of Cheap Food," *Time*, August 21, 2009.

Yvonne Zipp "The School Lunchroom Grows Green," *Christian Science Monitor*, May 29, 2009.

Index

Numerals

A

B

C

F

J

K

L

M

R

S

T